MAAS RAFF
AND
MAMA SYLVIE'S MANUAL
Life Lessons for Living Full

JAI

ABOUT THE AUTHOR

Jai is a Jamaican poet who for the last 23 years worked as an educator and restaurant operations leader. She now lives in Kentucky with her extended family. She is the mother of a 7-year-old boy who is the apple of her eye. Her story was born out of love for children compassion for their less-than-ideal situations that were by no means their fault. She honed her writing skills by documenting her life experiences. After teaching herself how to write poetry, she decided to embark on a journey to help others find their light at the end of the tunnel. Jai also has a passion for helping others and through her newly formed nonprofit, Sylvia's Hope Estate Inc., she focuses on families, especially children who have been undeserved or abandoned. Jai holds a degree in Psychology and Business from Keiser University, as well as a Master of Science degree in Human Resources and Organizational Development from the University of Louisville. This book is dedicated to the memory of Llewelyn and Sylvia Falconer.

JAI

MAAS RAFF
&
MAMA SYLVIE'S MANUAL

Lessons For Living Full
How It All Began...

Llewelyn Raphael Falconer was his birth name, I called him Mass Raff. That name meant more to me than I had ever imagined, since he was the first persons who gave me an insight into myself that even I could not see. He very jokingly mentioned that I would be an actor and Hollywood was my destination. And he did it in such a way that I believed him. My eyes were now set on achieving goals that I did not have any examples of in my environment to motivate it. But it felt real and achievable. He was my audience and my biggest cheerleader. He was a poetry lover and enjoyed reciting them around the glare of the bonfire we made from "cow dung" to keep mosquitoes at bay. His laughter was rare but infectious. A man of very few words, but when he spoke, his words were deep; a wealth of knowledge and brilliance beyond himself. Brilliance that he acquired only from the school called "life." He was an avid thinker, an excellent listener, and a very practical advisor. He was never born into a home with a father who would model manhood, yet he knew how to be a man and a father. His beginnings were humble – born out of wedlock in a modest home to a woman who adored him and a father who was ashamed of him. He grew up under less than favorable conditions and knew from early that hard work and perseverance were his only tickets. He married the love of his life, Sylvia/mama Silvie and their union produced seven children: five girls and two boys. He worked in the public sector as a truck driver until retirement, all the while doing his farming, which was his pride and joy.

"BUILD" was a key word for him. He constantly reminded me of how he used the stones life threw at him to make his castle. He lived in a one-bedroom house which he increased exponentially to seven by the time I came to know him. I often had the conversation about wanting to build a house but did not have enough money to do it all at once. He would only respond "one block at a time will bring it from one room to completion." I always had to draw the lessons from the statements, which made him even more intriguing to me. I admired him even more when I could not trace a point in his life when he had been given any "handouts" to build him or even involve himself in any illicit activities to make him who he was. The respect that flowed effortlessly from people who knew him was evidence that he had lived a life worthy of admiration.

Much is said about a successful man and his strong wife, and Mama Silvie was no exception. She was an average height full figured woman who walked with her back straight and her head held high. She had the most beautiful freckles on her face I had ever seen. Mama Silvie was the most selfless person I had ever met. I looked forward to Sunday evening at her house, whether it was to iron the uniforms for school, since we had no electricity at home, or simply just hanging out. She was a strict disciplinarian, and bedtime meant just that. She kept the home alive and lent of herself in all the ways she knew how, to all the people she could. We were close while she was alive. I remember seeing her cook huge pots of food and I would wonder why she did that, since there were only two of them living in the household. Back then, there was not any emphasis placed on cooking to refrigerate because they preferred freshly cooked food. Everything would be gone by the end of the day, and she would be happy to do it all over again the next day. I observed her one morning while I was with her. She got up every day before dawn and had her devotion. Then she would go to clean herself up in the bathroom and head straight to the kitchen. While she is preparing food, she is cleaning and organizing her house. After she was through with the house chores and the cooking, she would go to the front yard to sweep. By this, it would be daylight and people in the community would be up and about either going to work or school. If they ever said, "good morning," which everybody did, she would offer them breakfast. Much to my amazement, in no time the porridge was gone. School lunch was prepared in the same way and sometimes dinner. A dress maker by profession, but as the years went by; she practiced it less and less. The most sewing I have ever seen her done was at back-to-school time. She would buy fabric with her own money and sew uniforms for the kids in the community and surprise them with it.

In her later years, she got the opportunity to travel abroad to visit her adult children, and her trips were gift giving ones. Upon her return, the myriad of "stuff" that she brought back were distributed throughout the community, often leaving herself with nothing. Her usual disposition was always to do all you can to everyone that you can, for as long as you can. One trip stood out for me. This was when she planted a seed in me that sprang into action in that moment. We would excitedly hurry to see her the moment she landed at home. We knew that she was a "giver" and there would be something for everyone. On this occasion, she put aside "stuff" for others, and I felt neglected since I was not handed anything. So, I left the room feeling extremely disappointed. After a couple of minutes, I heard her yelling out my name, so I ran to her immediately. She was in the process of wrapping her brown leather suitcase in a bed spread. "This is my prized possession" she said. "I know that you are a girl who is going to achieve greatness and I want you to have this so you can use it when you start traveling the world." I was about nine years old at the time and did not understand what she was saying to me. My little mind was only content with the fact that I got something bigger in size than what everybody else got. She ushered me to the adjoining room and told me that she was going to put it on top of a wardrobe so when I was ready for it, I would know where to find it.

Months went by, and I would often retrieve my suitcase and wipe it down so the leather would not crack. That suitcase became my prized possession. I did not only treasure it for its physical characteristics, but its value was far greater; it represented – "A DREAM." A mere suitcase sparked a desire to explore the world's stage. Not only as a spectator, but as a person who earned a place there. Someone who would achieve whatever the mind was able to conceive.

My joys seemed short-lived when my aunt broke the news that my beloved Mama Sylvie was diagnosed with breast cancer. She had been ailing for some time with what she thought she could cure by using home remedies. She was also a spiritual woman and believed that there was nothing a prayer could not fix. I watched a tower of strength stripped one brick at a time, and it was painful. I only imagined her pain, but she did all she could to disguise it. The months following her diagnosis, she went to live with her daughter since she had lost mobility in her left hand. One day we came home from school to find the clothing line filled with clothes basking in the sun, as sparkling as can be. She sat on the veranda as usual. The helper was not there so we did not expect any such accomplishment. I did not ask any questions since kids never dared to question a grown up. My aunt came home and asked her about it. She boldly demonstrated how she did it. "I sat by the wash pan, use the good hand to put the clothes in the bad hand and rub it together until it was clean. Then I rinsed it with the good hand and use my teeth to help me to hold them while I hung them on the line." My aunt did not know whether to laugh or cry. Her stern warnings against household chores fell on deaf ears as sitting still was never part of her DNA. I imagined the torment she suffered when her body could not do what her mind wanted to do.

The house was my grandfather's property and had two apartments. By the time her body started to fail, the tenants had moved out and we moved over to the bigger apartment. Mama Sylvie and I shared a room (same bed) and my other two sisters shared the other room. She was an early sleeper and the chatter and laughter from my sisters' room often piqued my curiosity. She always made sure that we prayed together before we went to sleep. Her failing health bothered me, but I never expressed that to her. Her pain was suffered in silence. I would often dream that she left me alone in the room even when I knew she could not walk. I could never imagine going to sleep without her in the bed.

Cancer stole her away from me and my 13 years old self was angry with God. I had said so many prayers and begged for healing. It never came. But I could not understand why she remained so calm and faithful in the face of her failing health. I remembered our last conversation as if it were yesterday. We slept together during her final days. She always asked me to bring her some water, but this time she could not drink it sitting up, so I fed her with a straw. She looked at me and said in an extremely low tone, "God bless you. Do good to everyone you meet. If you cannot do good, then do not do anything." I knew that there were not going to be many more conversations after this. Her strength was waning, rapidly. I stared at her while she struggled to breath. Her shallow breaths seemed as if they were traveling through a war-torn land on flat tires that scraped against rusty steel beams. She barely gripped my hand, but I could still feel the warmth that came from her soul. I walked away knowing that I may never have the pleasure of lying beside her again. I was broken.

Saturday morning while mom swept the dried leaves off the lawn, and we watched cartoons, a familiar car sound rumbled in the distance. The closer it got, the more recognizable it became. It was the 1975 grey Hilman hunter that mass Raff had loaned my uncle. I began to eavesdrop just in time to hear "She died this morning" he said. Mommy held her stomach and wailed; a sound that burned through my entire being. I was not surprised, just disappointed. She transitioned as soon as we left for the weekend. Death had been a strange phenomenon to me and had only experienced its firsthand effects once before with Mamie (great grandmother). A few years had gone by, and I had forgotten about the darkness that I felt at her passing. She had told us that we should not be afraid because she would be protecting us. So, we felt like we had a guardian angel. Mama Sylvie's death felt different. She was 59 years old. How could a woman who did so much good be taken away so soon? Why did God allow that? How could I continue to believe when I saw her suffer when she didn't deserve it? I had so many questions and no answers.

OH DEATH

I've watched you growing inside of me
A crocked beast preparing for a delectable feast
Conflicted about your motives and blinded by your threats
You didn't birth me so my timeline you shouldn't intercept

The years are worn upon my wrinkled being
Regrets are wrapped up in my sleeves
I beg for release from this untimely rest
And keep vanishing beauty from my breast

Oh death save me from your mercy kill
Grant me an overflowing wish let it spill
Take this tumbling decay away
And restore the beauty of this perfect clay

The pain of life flows without restrain
Gift me this suffering withdraw your disdain
Don't play God to decide the time I leave
But if you must - kill me with kindness instead

If I got to choose the demons lurking in my path
I'd dispatch Satan's army to unleash on you their wrath
Grant me this great act of love though hard to commit
Of a lifetime free of you and all your despair

GRIEF

It was just yesterday we enjoyed exploring the reef
Such beautiful memories built though it was very brief
Time is a master, sometimes cruel, other times blissful disbelief
Today I sit on your monument broken, smiling at my grief

Oh gates of hell why do you open and dance for me
Must I prove that my love is greater than my vows
Till death do us part will never mean the same now
For the bosom of earth hugs closer than my love

All the daughters and sons you've stolen before
Isn't enough to quench your thirst and restore
The one God gave - a miracle you must conjure
This horror movie is just filled with gore

Now you've left me a blank
I pine in thoughts, deeds and actions fail to bank
Now my inner and out edges run down a slippery slope
Was this not love or was I meant to bleed?

We gathered at the family home. The silence broke with sniffles from my grandfather. This was the first time I saw my grandfather cry. My young mind could not fathom the likelihood, since in my eyes he was too strong for such a display of weakness. It was early morning, and his adult children came into his room to discuss plans for the burial. I sat at my vantage point on the far side of the verandah. My aunt started singing a hymn that she thought would be ideal for the service. It was one of Mama Slyvie's favorite. He spoke about her in ways I have never heard him utter. The hurt seemed overwhelming as he sat in his wooden chair by his door with his arms barely on the armrests. He slid back, tilted his head, that familiar sigh went up a notch and tears of a different language streamed down his face. I turned away just in time to catch a tear from the corner of my eye. I had no idea how to comfort him. How do you comfort a tower of strength? I did not think he ever needed a hug lest a shoulder to cry on. I watched him pull himself together as if he stepped out of a swamp unto dry land. They all agreed that it was not an enjoyable time to do this, as all eyes were blurred with tears. They relegated to rearranging bedroom furniture and turning over the mattress. This was traditionally done to prevent the "duppy" from recognizing the place and hence desist from visiting. I mourned my grandmother in my own way and preferred to think about her being in Santa Cruz while I visited home on a weekend.

There were two houses that mourned her. She had brought so much life to the home, that we almost forgot that she was ill. When we first went to live in town, she would visit occasionally and spent days on end to take care of us. We all crammed in the two-bedroom apartment. We slept wherever there was room and mam Sylvie made it her duty to wake us up at 5 am so we could grate boiled corn before we left for school. The task seemed daunting at first, but the fruits of the labor were enticing. We could barely wait for school to be dismissed so we could come home to corn pudding. Nobody could have done a better job.

The "nine night" lasted well over three weeks. Every night was a celebration leading up to the grand finale the night before the burial. I had never had the experience of such a huge gathering of people at the house at any one time. Each night saw unfamiliar faces as well as "resident guests" whose only motive was to eat and drink as much as they could get their hands on. She was loved by all who had the opportunity to meet her. The night before the funeral did not disappoint. I was looking forward to the singing, drumming and dancing of the "nine night group." Nine night is the Jamaican form of wake, except it is a much livelier celebration rather than a time of mourning. Traditionally, friends and family would gather at the home of the deceased and they would bring food and alcohol (white rum) to celebrate the life of the deceased with music (drumming), hymn singing and dancing. I anxiously awaited the start of the main event all dressed up and perched on the front step. However, I do not recall seeing anyone with anything in hand, let alone food. That part of the tradition was long forgotten. The night began at dusk and continued until daylight. Dinki-mini (a dance celebrating the creation of life) led to kumina (an invitation for the spirits of the person's ancestors to join and help the ghost to rest) and the women had their roles down pat. The drumming was mesmerizing, and before long I was gyrating as if possessed by one of the frolicking ancestors. A table was set in the middle of the tent with a few bottles of white rum. This was supposed to be done for the "duppy" who is believed to have joined the festivities. The patrons should wait until after midnight to drink or eat from the table as the "duppy" would have passed from this world into the next realm. The moment the crowd formed; the bottle seals broke. During the festivities, the dancers would periodically stop their prancing and demand rum or refuse to perform if their stock is not replenished. Friends and relatives helped to serve manish water (goat head soup) and sandwiches, fish and bread, white rice and curry goat and whatever food could suffice the hungry crowd. As the darkness left, so did the crowds. 4am came and the few patrons who were left kept watch until the morning sun drove drunkenness from their bodies.

For a moment I had forgotten that mama Sylvie died. It was funeral day and preparations were well underway. Smoke made its way high in the sky as the curry goat, manish water, white rice, fry chicken, stew beef and fry fish were prepared. This was for the repast. You never dared to have a funeral and not provide a haughty meal for the attendees. The black clothing on the bed was a stark reminder that the final day has arrived. I wore what I had – an over worn church dress with a big white bow tie, black shoes, and white socks up to my knees.

I very quickly realized that I was supposed to say my goodbyes as I saw her lay in the coffin. She had on her favorite dress and broad rim hat and looked as though she was sleeping. The viewing took place prior to the start of the service. They however decided to do another viewing at the grave side since the coffin could not fit in the grave that was made for it. The builders had underestimated the length of the coffin and made it a bit too short. They had to correct that problem, so they worked tirelessly to ensure that she was buried before sundown. It is believed that if the burial does not take place before dark, then it would have to be postponed. I never figured out where that came from, but I took the rebuilding time to say my goodbyes. I snuck up to the coffin when there was no one beside it. A small part of me was very afraid, but my heart nudged me to touch her. I starred for a moment. I wanted to make sure that she would not wake up or smile at me like she normally would. I needed one last touch just to convince me that she was gone. I did not realize that I was in so much denial and as my chest became heavier, I stretched my hand and laid it on hers. It was true…… she was stone cold and her soft skin as I knew it now feels like a piece of leather. What have they done to her? I thought. I could not cry but my chest wanted to burst open. I was not sure how long I was there because I didn't even hear the digging and flashing of concrete. I was only a few feet away from the tomb, but the silence felt as if I was in an airtight chamber; just the two of us. I thought she heard me when I said "bye mama Sylvie" because her hands felt warm for a moment. The singing continued the whole time and her 6'6" home was now ready for her. The men from the funeral home closed the coffin and I watched as they lowered my MAMA SYLVIE into her final resting place.

The celebration took my mind off the previous events, and once again life went on as usual. I did not see much of my grandfather in the next couple of days, but whenever I glimpsed him, he would be sitting in his favorite spot on the verandah appearing to be relaxed. I assumed he was ok. The days after the funeral proved to be the worst for me. For the first time, I realized that I had delayed reaction and when everyone else was over their mourning, mine had just begun. I found myself crying hysterically over amazingly simple things. The trips down to her house were once fun. Now, they felt like a death march. I could feel the heaviness of the air as I entered the once vivacious atmosphere. A usual happy walk to Mama Sylvie's house now became a burdensome one and I cried when mommy asked me to do it. No one realized what was happening to me and brushed it off as laziness. My tears spoke a language that no one understood. I imagined what she would say:

I Cried For You

I cried for you today
Knowing that I'm not able to stay
I watched you love me more than words can say
But I won't be able to spare your pain

I've lived the life that's been given to me
Had some great times and even sad times too
Half of my struggles I kept to myself
Just to enjoy you…my greatest love

When my golden heart stops beating
Know that I'm at rest
Don't cry as one with no hope
God always knows what's best

Today you will see my body for the last time
But my spirit will remain with you always
Treasure the memories we've made along the way
Until we meet again some day

Today it's farewell not goodbye my love
Be at peace with yourself
Death will put you to the test
But love is stronger than the rest

The days got easier as the sounds of summer strolled in. September came and facing the house was a terrifying thought. The room where we slept looked haunted and I was afraid to even go near it. My sisters and I followed each other around with each fighting for the middle. A mop stick fell in the passageway on one occasion, and it sounded like the echo of a haunted cave. We were frightened out of our skin, but after I realized that it was just the mop stick, I felt stupid. So, I braved up and stepped into "My room." My sisters looked on even more scared than I was. To my surprise, I felt more at ease than I have ever felt even when she was alive. The fear left and all I needed to get familiar with was the new arrangement of the furniture. A few days past and nothing happened. One morning my aunt beckoned to me that she was leaving for Kingston. I looked at the clock and saw that it was 5am. I pulled my cover and turned over on my side and tried to go back to sleep. As sleep eluded me, I periodically peeked at the clock to see how much longer I would need to be in the bed before daylight. I caught a shadow in the corner of my eye, so I turned to make sure of what I was seeing. Oh my god, I thought as fear crippled me. I knew that I was alone in the house because my other sisters were not there so who could that be. I tightly closed my eyes and reopened them just to make sure I was not dreaming. The perfect outline of "her" was coming toward the bed. Where is she going? I screamed in my mind. But I could not stand to look so I squeezed my eye lids together so tight that my eyeballs felt as if they were going to burst any minute. My bed angled as if someone had just sat on it. My heart fought to stay alive, and its throbbing moved my body towards the wall. "Lord help me" I tried to whisper, but the words could come out. The bed sprung back to its normal height, and I waited for what seemed like forever before I opened my eyes. I slowly opened one eye and hoped that only the darkness was staring back at me. I was alone again, and my heart was glad. I prayed my "strength" prayer and hoped it worked. 1992 came and went and so did all the fears of duppies.

Mourning the loss of his love was an arduous task for my grandfather. He not only lost her physical presence, but also everything else. Until now, he never had to pick out his own clothing, prepare his meals or even decide how to coordinate his colors. He struggled with mealtime and although he could have a house cleaner, he decided against it. Mommy took over the task of feeding him and ensured that he had clean clothes. My sisters and I would go by his house on the weekends to clean up. Mama Sylvie was no longer around to ensure that we went to church and there was no other pull, so we stopped. He buried himself in work, both on his farm and at the job. He was a few years from retirement but was not looking forward to it. It appeared as if he spoke more to himself than people. His regular visit to his friend Mr. Salmon was his enjoyment.

Retirement came and as expected, he did not know what to do with himself. He visited the pastures just to look at it and it appeared as if he waited for a leaf to fall in the yard so he could pick it up. The house saw him less even though there was more time to relax. He became friends with the trees and took turns visiting them. He was once a cattle farmer, so he owned lots of land. My fondest memory of his farm was at tamarind season. I was a climber, and my sisters could barely get past the low hanging limbs. I enjoyed sitting in the tree to "stuff my gut." If they were nice to me, then I would pick some for them. If not, I sit and enjoy myself before feeling sorry for them and throwing them some. There was a tank by his small one room house/hut on the property which had fish in it. He would teach us how to catch the fish and if we were lucky, we could cook it. I enjoyed herding the cows and counting them to ensure all were accounted for. With every visit, the number got bigger. Thieves often helped themselves to his cattle but not without a fight. His "one pop" as we affectionately named his shot gun was his best friend. They ventured on daily 3 am trips on foot along the over three-mile journey. After a while, due to several circumstances, the numbers dwindled significantly and before long, there was only land without cattle.

The over 70 acres of land became his playground. Its pristine pedicured appearance caught the eyes of the organizers of the "Champion farmer" competition and we were soon off to the Independence show ground in Denbigh Clarendon where he would receive the coveted title. That trophy accompanied him even to the United States embassy when he applied for a visa. That's how proud he was of his accomplishments. Anyone who would listen, heard about it as it played like a broken record. He defended his title in the subsequent three years and retained it with pride.

He was my "go to" person when I was in college and had essays to write. Any topic was one he could argue. My debates lived on the back of his insight. All I needed to do was give him enough time for the "inspiration" to come. He said he only worked off "inspiration" because that was the only time his thoughts would flow. So, I would call him to give heads up and then visit with my pen and paper in hand ready to take notes under the old cherry tree at the side of the house. He never wrote any scripts. He spoke freely and if I missed a word, he would not remember what he had said. The speech almost never followed a logical order, but the points were powerful. "Where did you learn all of this?" I would ask. "Ha ha ha" he chuckled. "I only went to grammar school, but university graduates cannot do what I do." I nodded in agreement. After the public speaking class, I would pick his brain about current affairs and newsworthy items. He was a staunch "Laborite" and would very readily criticize the government for gross mismanagement of the country that he loves. TV was only to watch the news and the radio talk shows were a major part of passing his day.

My job took me across the Island, and I would often drive the 15-mile journey to pick him up so he could "roll" with me. "Man, get ready by 8 am tomorrow we're going to May Pen." "8 you said." "Yes." "OK see you tomorrow." I knew that he would be up and ready by 6am so I dare not be late. I knew that I would need to provide him with his meals before I brought him back home. "Ms. T, you grandfather said he's hungry" yelled a staff member. "Again! Time to take him home. This is his third plate." I said under my breath. If a week ever went by without an invitation to travel, the call would come. "Miss Jan, are you coming to pick me up anytime soon?" "Yes Man I'll come get you tomorrow."

He enjoyed sitting in the restaurant and striking up conversations with the patrons. Before the day was over, he would find someone to talk politics with. During our journeys, our conversations were fulfilling and insightful. Anything was a good speaking point, and nothing was out of bounds. His advice was deep and often pushed my brain into overdrive.

"Never step on anyone while you climb the ladder called life. You'll fall faster than the time it took you to climb and pass the same person you hurt on your way down" he said.

Then as quickly as he finished saying it, he stopped talking. He never elaborated if it was not required. He caught me off guard when he mentioned that I was an exceptionally good driver. I did not think he was observing me so closely because I did not see his head turned towards me at any point. I accepted the compliment as I consciously performed cautious maneuvers around the sharp corners along mountainous terrain.

"I can't believe what I have come to" he constantly repeated as age did an intricate dance with him. The enlarged heart never bothered him much, except with the swollen feet when the socks are too tight. Numerous attempts to get him a companion at home failed and I stopped asking. Once or twice a week I would check on him to make sure he's ok. On one of our weekly trips, unexpectedly he said:

"Choose carefully when you are looking for a partner. When poverty comes through the door, love jumps through the window."

I stood in silence while it resonated in my head to the extent of disquiet. Why would he say that? What did he notice about my love life? Was he paying that much attention? I know he knew my significant other but was not sure how much he knew about him. I nodded in agreement and asked no further questions. My head's diary took a note in capital letters because I knew there was soundness in his advice. My job now is always to know when to draw on them.

His reputation was particularly important to him, and he often uttered phrases such as

"Show me your friend and I'll tell you who you are."

He has never been implicated in any legal issues and tried his hardest to stay away from breaking the law. In fact, he was very respectful of the law and made every effort to educate himself on them. His mode of dress and the way he spoke suggested that he was judgmental about people who chose to carry themselves unkempt. He was not a showoff and was very modest with most things. The hair must be cut (even though I had to do it), the shirt must be tucked, even if it was dirty and your walk needs to be upright. That to me spoke to his character.

He was 79 years old and plans were in the making for his 80th birthday celebration. His spirit took a dip as his appetite changed and he yearned for the companionship of family. I would often let him sleep by my house so he would not' be so lonely.

I had just parked my van in the parking lot at one of my locations and headed upstairs to start my daily routine. My phone started ringing. I glanced at the screen and saw that it was daddy calling me. I went to the office to answer so I could get a little privacy and quietness. "Janice I just found Mass Raf dead" he blurted in a trembling anxious voice. "What did you say?" "I saw him yesterday morning, but I didn't stop in the evening. I came by and went to the back and found him in the garage." My feet indicated that it would not be able to hold up my weight much longer, so I sat down. The tears flowed immediately. I told him that I would be there in a few minutes and hung up the phone. The usual 40 minutes journey was cut in half, literally.

Nothing could have prepared me for what I was about to see. A few people from the community had gathered. I walked pass them and went to the spot. He lay there on his back across the doorway with the hands above his head. As I stared in disbelief, I wondered who did this to him. I had no authority on any such field, but my first instinct was foul play.

The police came and did their routine "look." A few days later, the authorities contacted me to inform me that they had scheduled an autopsy for the following week, and they needed a representative. I agreed to make myself available. I quickly reprimanded myself for such a decision as I was not sure if I would be able to watch them "cut him up." I immediately began to mentally prepare myself through self-talk:

"You need to know what happened so this is the process."

"he would have wanted you to follow through with this."

"He always told you to stand up for what you believed in."

"Do not disappoint him now."

As I drove to the public morgue, I imagined the coroner slicing through my Mass Raf and tears welded up in my eyes.

"I cannot back out now, I had already committed to it, so I had to show up. It is going to get done with or without you so your presence would cause them to behave respectfully towards him."

As I parked, I glanced in the direction of the police officer, and he greeted me with a nod. I went over to him and asked where the autopsy would take place. He informed me that they were running behind so as soon as they are ready, they would call me. After a 30 minutes wait, he came to my vehicle and told me to follow him. My palms suddenly began to sweat as I approached a building along the side of the hospital property. I nervously peeked inside and glimpsed Mass Raf on the stainless-steel table. I chickened out immediately and my first thought was to run. But, I remembered all the conversations I'd had with myself, and I took one more step closer. The officer encouraged me to come closer "he's dead so he won't feel a thing" he said. I wanted to fight him as he chuckled. The coroner's assistant raised his clever and I felt as if it went through my heart. I could not watch so I told the coroner to do his checks and inform me of the findings after he has finished chopping him up. I shirked every time the clever hit a bone, but I could not bring myself to leave either. It could not have been more than 15 or 20 minutes, but it felt like a lifetime. I heard their conversation, and it sounded like they were out to lunch. I grew angrier by the minute and welcomed the sound of completion "Ok maam, like I said he had a heart attack." "I need to speak to the coroner" I responded. "No problem." "Doc, what are your findings?" He explained what I already knew. "What about the bruises on his face?" I protested. "These are surface bruises and may have happened as a result of handling, see" using his knife to cut away the skin. The blood drained from my face, and it took everything out of me not to lose it. The messy sewing of the flesh on his chest formed the shape of a "Y" and the only question in my mind was "Why." Defeated, I collected the report and left the building. "Did I ask enough questions?" "Had I done enough?" "Did I give up too easily?" "Did the coroner collude with the officer to cover their ineptitude? I was hard on myself, but I tried. I suggested an independent coroner but that was going to be an uphill battle, so we decided to move ahead with burial plans.

By now, I had become an experienced funeral planner. My emotions, though expressed, were not allowed to run wild. I took a three week break from work so I could execute the plan. The airport runs, funeral home visits and government office appointments kept me busy the whole time. Mass Raf had started going to church and became a member of the Balaclava Seventh Day Adventist church. He never missed a Sabbath service and his regular seat longed for his warmth. 17 years after Mama Sylvie's death, I was reliving the same experience. This time tough I understood death to be a part of life with all its complexities, and that too shall pass. Plans were being made to celebrate his 80th birthday. Little did we know that he would be gone just a few months before? I celebrated his life because he lived. I celebrated him because he gave of himself – if only to me. I respected his "dash" because he made sense of it even when the odds stacked up high against him. So, without regrets, I said my goodbyes to my mentor, my "ride or die," my advisor, my life tutor. One of the poems Henry Wadsworth Longfellow penned and he frequently repeated reminds me of his life:

The heights of great men reached and kept

Were not attained by sudden flight

But they while their companion slept

Were toiling upwards through the night.

I thought about him constantly and what he would do in certain situations. His life lessons were indelibly printed in my mind. I thought about his relationships with other people, or his lack thereof. He was a "loner." One who works relentlessly to achieve what is important to him; one who believes in coaching people to be their best self; one who may not know how to verbally or even physically express emotions, but you can rest assured that he is going to come through at the appointed time. He was adept at introspection. "That's what makes a man grow" he would say.

If I were to imagine that I am being divinely guided, it would be by Mama Sylvie and Mass Raff. This compilation of life lessons is a reminder that we do not exist by ourselves. Therefore, one should share their knowledge for others to grow.

LIFE LESSONS PT 1

Everything happens at the right time.
Be patient.

There is a reason for everything. Though we may not yet come into the knowledge of these truths, we may never be able to understand why night follows day or why nature's clock operate with a rhythmic motion that sprouts buds and blooms colors. Some things are predictable, some are random. Some may never be revealed. In this era of information overload, many occurrences will be explained. Whenever they present themselves, it is the right time. The story is told of the farmer sowing seeds. He knows when to till the soil, when to put the seeds in the ground, when to fertilize, and when to water. He may have the experience to understand the process of the crop, but the rest is outside of his control. It does not matter how impatient he gets; he must follow the process if he wants to achieve remarkable results. Timing is everything. The same is true for all aspects of our lives. When we do what is required, the results will follow. And if it does not turn out as planned, we get anxious and frustrated. Finding the formula for a great crop may take several rounds of practice to perfect it. There is no such thing as overnight success. The work must be done.

Life Lessons Pt 2

Every town has a mascot, and every family has a cruff (uninspired person).

Life is a colorful mosaic filled with pieces to make up how we experience it. There are some things that may seem strange for those who are living through them. Your experience may feel unique to you, but there are others who experience the same. We experience a blend that makes life what it is. It is through connections we realize that others may have experiences that make our seem like a walk in the park. Then this knowledge creates a network where our humanness can be understood, supported, respected, and celebrated.

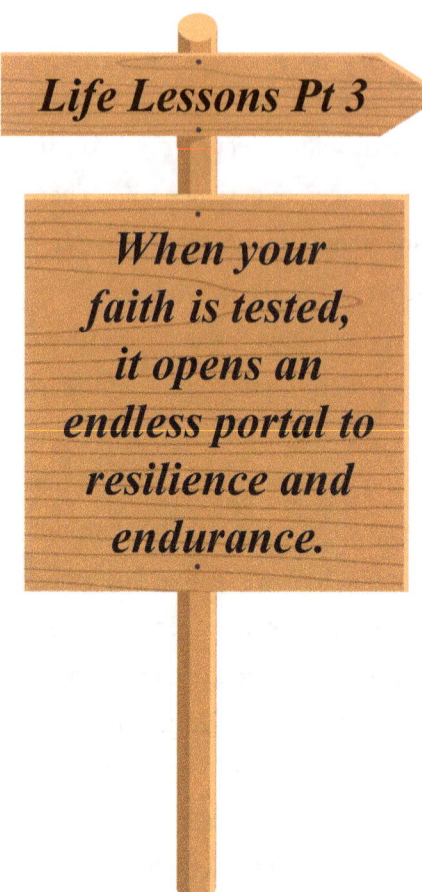

Life Lessons Pt 3

When your faith is tested, it opens an endless portal to resilience and endurance.

We all have a built-in survival mechanism. Like different models of cars, the features run the gamut of strength and endurance. However, a custom-built car can be manufactured to specification based on individual preferences. The final product may not be easily achieved since it must go through crash testing, resistance, and other refining processes. These processes may be time consuming and often seem like failure. But the result will hold endless possibilities. We may never know what we are made of until situations present themselves that requires us to perform a crash test. And the effects may be devastating. But although our strength is tested, it does not mean that we should give up. Go back to the drawing board. You will surprise even you because you did not know what power sleeps within. It is part of the refining process that leads to your purpose. If you choose not to tap into your goldmine, then your life becomes meaningless.

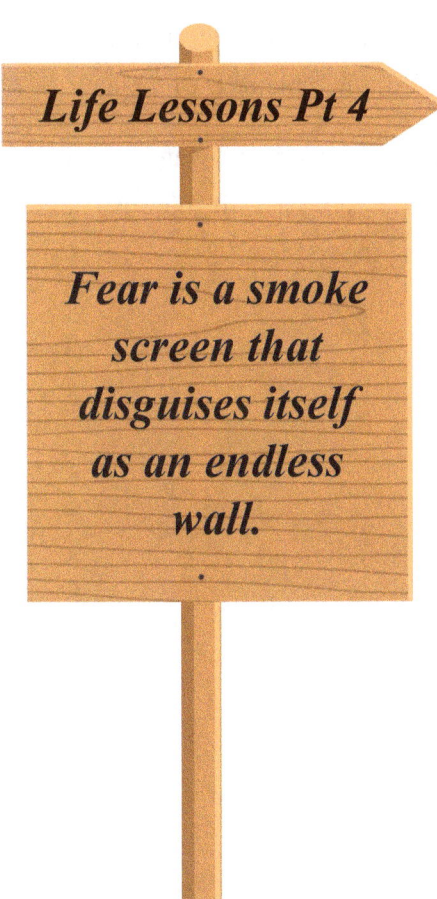

Life Lessons Pt 4

Fear is a smoke screen that disguises itself as an endless wall.

Fear can be crippling. The unknown can prevent you from taking a single step or feel like you are drowning in a waterless ocean. Everything that was leaned may be lost in a moment of fear. We over-think, under utilize our experiences, and freeze. The inertia can be temporary or could last a lifetime. Getting past the debilitating effects of fear may mean diving into that ocean without a life jacket. Maureen was already in her forties and had been driving since she was twenty years old. She was an exceptionally good driver, but harbored the worst fear of driving over the rail less bridge that connected the major cities. She would park her car and travel by public transportation whenever she had to go into the capital. I could see the sweat bursting through her pores when she was telling me that she would NEVER drive over that bridge. But "can't" was not a part of my vocabulary. So, I started coaching her to open her eyes to what she is capable of. Finally, she decided to do it. I was so proud of her. But she panicked when she saw the bridge. She called me and hysterically announced that she will not be able to do it. Sometimes we need a reminded of how to open that storage box. And at the sound of my voice, she went through the steps, turned the key, and unleashed her strength. From the other side of the bridge, she screamed so loudly, my ears went partially deaf for the remainder of the day.

Remember, you have a lifeguard who walks on water and will reach into the depths of the ocean to find you. That lifeguard is within you. Never stop searching until you find them.

Life Lessons Pt 5

Lying to others may get you through a few gates. Lying to yourself will make you a prisoner behind gates.

My name is (fill in name), and I am an (fill in the wall you built, eg. Alcoholic, drug addict, etc). This may seem like a simple statement, but it is in fact one of the most powerful statements you will ever see. It forces you to sit with yourself and look at the truth. Sitting with yourself is never easy. It may feel like torture for some. Admitting who you are is the first step towards realizing who you can become. But you must conquer self before you can claim victory over other things. When you know who you are and do not like who you are, then efforts will be made to change to a better version of yourself. However, when you like the person you are, endless possibilities are unlocked, and then you will have a shorter, easier journey to becoming your best self. It takes courage to start this journey. And even higher dosages to endure. This person should be the most authentic, unique you who will not apologize for releasing themselves from their self-imposed prison.

LIFE LESSONS PT 6

Feed what's feeding you. Only a fool kills the source of his food.

The Bible reminds us of the stages in our lives and "normal" behaviors for such stages.

"When I was a child, I spake as a child, I understand as a child, I thought as a child: but when I became a man, I put away childish things (1 Corinthians 13:11 KJV)."

One of the responsibilities that comes with adulthood is providing for those who are dependent on us. Whatever the means for that provision (job, self-employment, etc.), one must protect that source/s so that they will continue to be in a good place. Circumstances may derail the plans, but when one willfully disrupts the source of his livelihood, the repercussions may not be enjoyable. Having no backup plan for unforeseen circumstances may plunge the situation into further disrepair. Deciding what is priority #1 and taking steps to ensure that behaviors are aligned with that priority is necessary to achieving success. Put time and effort behind the thing that affords you a good life. If it is the job, give it 100%. If it is your own business, give it 100%. The return on your investment will be great.

Life Lessons Pt 7

A mother's prayers and tears speak the language of angels.

Sometimes it is not because of what you have done that determines your abundance. It is in spite of who you are. It is who is interceding on your behalf. There are parents and grandparent who will relentlessly plead for you, even when you do not deserve it. Sometimes they do not wish for themselves the same abundance that they do for you. But they will be fulfilled by witnessing blessings being bestowed upon you.

A Mother's Love

Her full time schedule clashes with the part time grind
Sleepless nights and round the clock fights
With little warriors flexing muscles to show their might
She knows sometimes and sometimes she knows not
But through it all, she wears the honor of a mother's love.

Her innate abilities a mind blowing mystery
Her intellect and courage passed down through history
Her heart's constitution surpasses her petite stature
Voluntary love presentations, expecting no compensation
Woman you deserve the honor of a mother's love.

Those scars on your body looks great on you
Representing your strength and courage to pull through
Rips and tears many would kill for, some never endured
Misery, affliction, and adversity carried so gracefully
Woman, you deserve the honor of a mother's love.

So Today, and everyday moving forward
When you think to describe her as diminished
Her body fights as serotonin tries to take flight
Multitasking, skills mastery to her delight
And like the rock of Gibraltar she stands built
Woman, wear your crown like the queen that you are
Cause Only you know the price of a mother's love!

Life Lessons Pt 8

A thief will never rob an empty building.

Whenever you accumulate value (physical or otherwise), jealousy and envy will cause others to pursue you with ill intent. The devil does not waste time on empty vessels. Be mindful of that always, but do not allow that to dim your light.

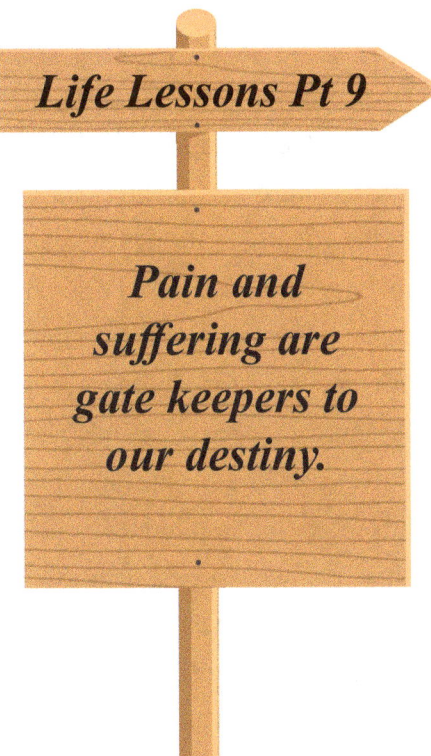

Life Lessons Pt 9

Pain and suffering are gate keepers to our destiny.

Pain and suffering are gate keepers. They guard the gates to your success. Some will never cross because they are scared to sweat and bleed. Failure to tap into your strength limits your jackpot. Resilience is heightened when the jackpot is huge. Whatever is value will be fought for with everything you have. This fight may seem irrational to many, but your fight won't always be understood. It is personal. Pain does not feel good. We live our lives trying to avoid it, but if you feel it, then it means you are alive. Be grateful!

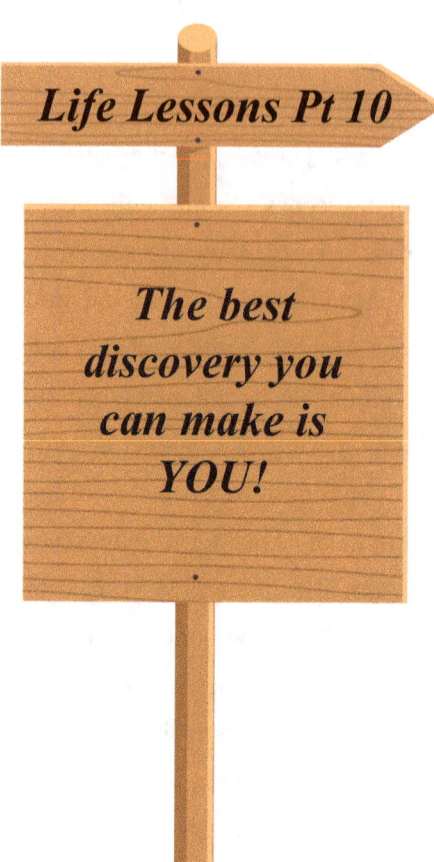

Life Lessons Pt 10

The best discovery you can make is YOU!

You are a powerful spiritual being with direction and purpose. Recognizing that is the first step to finding you. Discovering who you are is a deliberate and personal journey. The experiences on that path may leave scars because you may not like what you find. The journey provides for healing time and when all requirements are achieved, one will experience the best version of themselves. Then you will not have to tell anyone about your self-acceptance, they will see it.

Life Lessons Pt 11

Our mind is to us as a toolbox is to a mechanic.

The mind is the most powerful tool one can possess. Though sometimes difficult to define, it encompasses our thoughts, intelligence, will, and all conscious and unconscious mental activities. It is the place where life happens. Our gifts and talents are projected from that place. Like a mechanic, one must work with the right tools to perform the job. A mechanic guards his tool, keeps them in good condition, and invests in them so he can enjoy the return on his investment. The seat of our experience lies within our minds. How we treat with it determines how we experience life.

LIFE LESSONS PT 12

You must learn to appreciate silence to hear your own voice.

The noise of everyday life can be deafening. We are constantly bombarded with a myriad of methods and ways to accomplish a task.

We are taught to look outside of ourselves for the answer to everything. And everything comes in attractive packages. Deciphering the trash from the prize may be a daunting task for some, and an impossible one for others. It is necessary to break from the conundrum and retreat into solitude. There you will have autonomy over what you ingest. You can guard yourself from the attacks and build your defensive strategies. It is there you will realize that there's a teacher within you that has all the answers to the questions. It is there that you will find yourself.

Life Lessons Pt 13

Give without an expectation to receive.

There always seem to be a race for accumulation of resources. The goal is for little to become much and much to become greater. When much is given, much is expected. But because of the scarcity mindset, some refuse to let go of the treasures that they have amassed. Whatever these treasures (knowledge, physical possessions), they will die with you if it is welded within your grips. It is control that allows us to be selfish with our gifts. Within reason, one must pay it forward. Someone invested in you. Invest in someone else. You are not being asked to give until you go broke. You are asked to help someone along your journey. There is always someone on the end of the good you do that is better because of what you do! They do not always voice that. Do not be discouraged when you get no accolades. Do it because it is the right things to do.

I GIVE

The pieces of me I chose to share
Are unusually strange that's why you stare
An open heart for all who dare
To challenge a love as raw and rare

I speak aloud though none would hear
I walk long distances without fear
I carry burdens that's hard to bear
I give it all for you my dear

No ulterior motives or strings attached
For in my spirit you were the perfect match
The door was always left unlocked
So be content with what you've got

I give of myself to stem the tides
When the belly of the beast is open wide
Love and generosity will calm the storm
Providing warmth for one or all

Life Lessons Pt 14

Actions speak louder than words.

A snake only shed its skin to become a bigger snake. They are who they are. No matter how different they look, their nature is still the same. Do not be fooled by people who claim change. Change should be a noticed transformation without reverting to old ways of being. If the new behaviors are temporary, then genuine change has not occurred. Change is a process and must be given time and effort. When the goal is achieved, you will know. Their actions will speak louder than their words.

Life Lessons Pt 15

Idle talk is a sin.

Not everything deserves a response. Some people will not appreciate your silence and may never value your words. Do not waste your time trying to convince them. Respect the stage where they are at and recognize that they may not be at your level. If they are willing to learn, teach them. If not, give them time to realize their ignorance. Run from empty conversations, hate & gossip. Do not drink poison because you are thirsty. Know who you are. That is all that matters.

Life Lessons Pt 16

It only takes a few minutes for someone to nail you to the cross in their mind or put you on a pedestal.

People rely on their experiences to help them make sense of the world. Some experiences are negative, and the result is flawed. Your appearance may not fit into their limited knowledge, you may have qualities that they lack, and you may be more successful. For those reasons and more, not everyone will like you. In fact, some will hate you without knowing anything about you. That is their loss. What is important is that you love and respect you. Everything else will resolve itself.

Life Lessons Pt 17

Every accomplishment is achieved because of a decision to start.

I wanted to build a house, but I did not have the money it would need to bring it to completion. I had just started saving money and did not want to get back to not having money. After a conversation with Mass Raff, I walked away with a plan that would allow me to meet my goals where my finances could afford. His advice was "you cannot achieve anything unless you start." Sometimes the plan is not perfect or maybe there is no plan, but you must start. So, the steps were broken down into manageable one, and the clarity that I received allowed me to see hope. A journey of a million steps begins with the first step.

LIFE LESSONS PT 18

There are no problems, only opportunities.

Every day we are faces with different scenarios from which to choose. The choices we make will have either a positive or negative impact on us or someone else. Choose carefully. When faced with tough situations, choose to look at the glass half full instead of half empty. Then stretch your brain to find the other half. When you begin each day with a "can do" outlook, the resolution to the puzzles will present themselves. Too often we see roadblocks instead of roadways. Our brain will only respond the way we train it. Stalling time should be thinking time. New creations should come from your old obstacles. Our broken pieces should be used to make a masterpiece.

BROKEN PIECES

Extraordinary beauty lies
Where broken pieces reside
Growing anew from the earth
Evolving through various stages from birth
Torn apart then built up
In broken pieces lies the good stuff

It's incandescent masterpiece
Appeared full and complete
Perfect in every way
But as such was never meant to stay
The cracks of circumstances and vile attacks
Refines it aglow with ardor that's exact

The whispers round about it hear
Sprinkles lightly spotted dust to smear
Slowly covering its glow
Until energy forgets to flow
The morning will usher anew
Til bursts of light begins to shine through

Embrace the broken pieces of you
For these are the parts that carry you through
The trauma that you refuse to face
Is the treadmill to speed up your pace

Give it a voice so it can speak
Then sit back and watch it peak

Boldness will awaken in her eyes
Resonate even with those who despise
Occurring repeatedly strengthening her strides
Killing the putrid stench of bloodlines
Emerging rejuvenated from the ash
Newness of beauty shining like cash

Life Lessons Pt 19

Some of the loudest barks have no bite.

Things are not always the way they seem. People often try to mask their insecurities by pretending to be who they are not. Dogs will bark loudly at other animals that they fear to scar them off. Similarly, barking owls make "barking" sounds that may allow one to think the sounds are coming from a dog. We tend to make associations based on what we already know. But we are not always right. Loudness does not mean strength and quietness does not mean weakness. People will "talk the talk" but when required, they cannot "walk the walk." Conversely, there are others who are capable but prefers to be quiet about it. One must be able to assess a situation at a deeper level than what the surface presents. Engaging all the senses is required to be able to make accurate judgments. It is only then that one will have a true picture of what they are up against.

Life Lessons Pt 20

You may bring the donkey to the well, but you cannot force it to drink.

We often fool ourselves into thinking that we can change people's behaviors and thought processes. While we may be able to apply tactics that produces temporary results, they may revert to old habits when the circumstances are different. People will change when they see value in changing. Forcing someone to do something that they do not want to do is not the best way to help them. However, when they are convinced, the change will happen. Use the power of influence instead.

Life Lessons Pt 21

Opportunity is a lonely old person if it does not have action as its companion.

There is power in opportunity, but one will only be successful if they do what is required to bring it to life. There is one major difference between a self-made person and one who received hand down. The difference is commitment! These people do not understand the value of a process because they never had to do the work. Those who have had to methodically plan and execute the means to an end will have a sense of accomplishment, and therefore have a greater level of appreciation for the rewards. It takes more than a wish to get results. Unless you believe in magic. Physical, mental, emotional, and psychological considerations all go into acting on an opportunity. It can be draining. But it will all be worth it.

Life Lessons Pt 22

Sometimes you must be willing to unlearn things to be better.

The world is a huge place with a myriad of cultures and methods of learning. One may be able to survive comfortably in their neighborhood if they choose to remain there. The learnings from their environment may be sufficient to continue their traditional path. Growth does not happen in your comfort zone. There is a reason we grow physically when we are asleep…. it is painful. Discomfort is sometimes the best thing that could ever happen to you. I do not pray for my enemies to be removed. They are my motivation. If they are gone, I would get too comfortable.

Venturing into an unfamiliar environment may be challenging for them and their comfortability will be severely affected. Survival has now taken on a new meaning. The food that they are accustomed to eating may not be available. The language may be unfamiliar. Their security in themselves and what they know may not be sufficient to get them to achieve the simple pleasures of life. A choice is presented here. Either return to the nest or learn the new ways of life. Returning home may be the easier one to make, but it may not be the best decision for them to grow. Sometimes the path we take forces us to become the best version of ourselves. That may break you and picking up the pieces may be devastating, but the person you will build from those pieces is going to be a powerhouse.

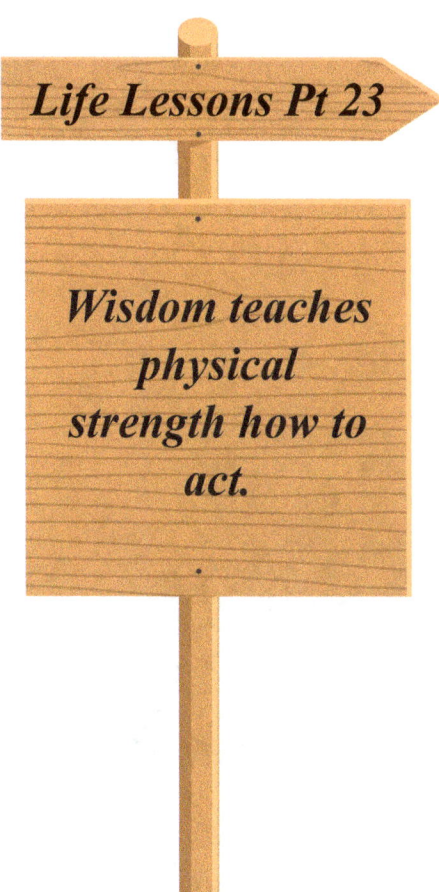

Life Lessons Pt 23

Wisdom teaches physical strength how to act.

Youthful exuberance can be a troublemaker. As a young adult, it was easy to stay up all night and party for days on end. Then go to work as if I had a full eight hours of sleep. In my mind, I had endless strength and energy. I did not understand the value of pacing myself. I had not begun to feel the strain that I was putting on myself. Although I was not physically tired at the time, my body started giving me a few cues that caused me to listen. After that wakeup call, I learned that everything will always be here, and everything does not have to be done at once. As one gets older, they should get wiser. They should learn that there are better ways to accomplish life's goals without sacrificing themselves. They should learn that they can redirect their energy towards more important things now to reap greater rewards later. They will learn that being present and enjoying life does not mean killing themselves.

LIFE LESSONS PT 24

Show me your friends and I will tell you who
you are!

A friend use to mean a person who is attached to another by an
emotional string. Love was the glue that bonds them together. They had

similar interests and would "look out" for each other. Social media has butchered that meaning. Now, there are friends that we have never met or even had a conversation with. Let us stick to the traditional meaning for the purpose of this explanation. If one is to wear the friend label, they should be familiar; such that I know they are worthy to share a part of me with. I may not know everything about them, but I should know enough to make a friendship determination. I should be proud of our association, because it aligns with my idea of who I am. Although there are some friends who fit this definition better than others, each friend should have a similar character. It is often said that we attract who we are. If that is true, then my friends should not be a notorious criminal when I am a law-abiding citizen. Family members are not our choice, friends are. One can determine your morals based on what you support.

BRIDGE OF LIFE

One foot in front of the other
One step that puts us closer
One memory etched in time
On this trek we'll never forget

As a babe we enter the race
Some choosing to go at a slow pace
Storms will rage and threaten your gaze
But they will always clear the way

Many will tread the same path
Others will approach it with pure wrath
Expectations broken will cause
Teeth and tongue to get distraught

Oh, bridge of life how will I cross?
When troubled waters seem to pass
So, near your mouth I will not last
Lest it swallows my aching heart

One step farther from the start
Friendships made along its path
To encourage and strengthen one and all
Lighten the load and give a good laugh

Towards the end there is a mark
Very different from where you start
Take your final bow happy as a lark
For the bridge of life, we all have to cross

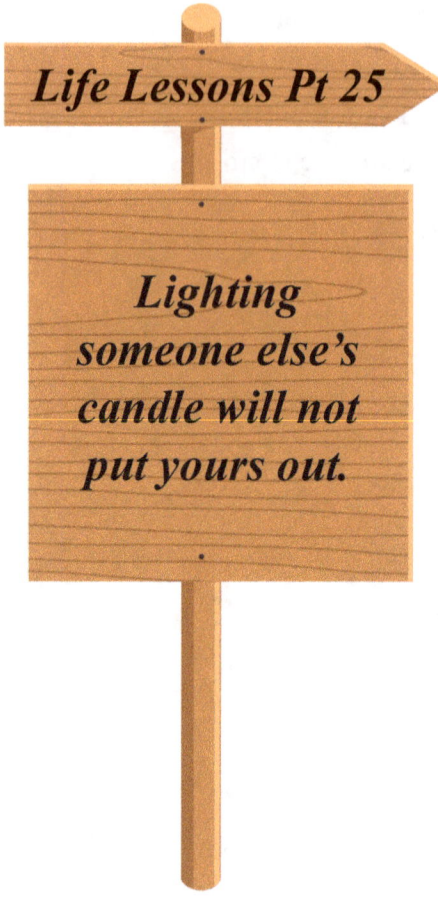

Life Lessons Pt 25

Lighting someone else's candle will not put yours out.

Mama Sylvi lived an exemplary life of lighting others' candles. She, like Tabitha of Joppa, was full of good works. It was easy for her to share what she had so that others could survive. The needy found her, and her coffers were never empty. She gave not from her material abundance, but from the little she had. She fulfilled her purpose.

No one should be forced to share. It should be done from the heart. But the option should not be to throw away resources that can be fuel for someone in need. You can afford to buy it, but it does not mean you have the right to waste it. There are millions of people who would do anything for a bite of food. Find someone to help.

The more candles you light, the brighter the atmosphere will become. It not only makes life colorful, but it also prepares you for more abundance that is to come. The key to living in abundance is to give. That is the only way to release your fear of lack. Try it, then watch abundance return 10-fold. Everyone wants miracles. Even those who are fortunate. But if you do not get your miracle, you can be one to someone else less fortunate than you. The smallest of gestures can mean the world to someone. Pay it forward!

TIME BOUND

Some never find it
Some were determined to fight it
Many started and never finished it
Few choose to listen to it
For those who never found it
Miserable lives and yearnings filled it

It burns like a fire
Only purposeful action can quench it
It stings like a bee
The venom of jealousy is no match
It comforts like the hand of God
Follow through and just watch

The pendulum of purpose swings left and right
You must stay grounded to experience its delight
Masking fools seek to plunge you in a plight
Killing your passion for the thing that is right
Try as they may they can never put out your light
Remember dark spaces only illuminate your might

The creator formed you and placed you in that body
It may scare you when you find that it's just your vessel
The one job you got is to transform competing energies
So don't get distracted by what you attract, you're extraordinary

Don't seek profit over what is greater than even you
Never forget the master cause your purpose is time bound.

Life Lessons Pt 26

For every great victory, there is a great sacrifice.

Everyone that has ever entered your life served a purpose, but they were not all meant to stay. They either showed you the worst part of you, or the best part of you. You are the sum of every person you ever met. Choose well what you keep and who you discard. The cycle of life may be difficult to understand, but there are several things we cannot control. We were born into families we did not choose. From the moment we were born, the death clock started ticking. Along our path, we find people who will either be friend or foe. Foes are easy for us to separate from. But friends and family members are hard to detach. Sometimes these situations may cause a lifetime of emotional and physical harm. However long it takes, whenever the time is right, the cycle will be complete. Then one must learn how to cope. Destiny is a womanizer….it leaves behind victims. Do not feel guilty if the person who was most helpful to you on your journey, was not there to witness and enjoy your success. They played their part. Be grateful. But be careful not to willfully use others for what they can do for you. Life always comes full circle.

Your challenges are not your enemies. They are there to pull your strength, talent, and perseverance out from deep within you. So, when you are challenged, do not throw in the towels on your dreams. Choose instead to sacrifice that small, nagging voice in your head that says you won't ever win. You have the power to do more than you can ever imagine. Do not underestimate yourself.

Life Lessons Pt 27

Know who you are!

You are not a victim… regardless of what was done to you.
You are not what you have been through.
You are not who they say you are.
You are not going to stoop to the level they want you to go to.
You are fearful and wonderfully made.
You are a gift from God.
You are a queen.
You are a king.
So, act like it!

Life Lessons Pt 28

Learn to trust yourself first.

Everyone has trust issues. Many of the issues are a projection of what is going on within. Others are developed from experience. But there is also an innate instinct colors what trust looks like. It takes a while before a child can trust anyone other than its parents. Trust does not come automatically for most people. It is hard to build, but when broken, it can take a lifetime to mend. Unrealized expectations can create a world wind effect that may spiral out of control if not recognized and treated.

An understanding of who you are will allow you to have faith in yourself. A healthy perception of self will create more channels for trusting others.

Life Lessons Pt 29

Life is your best personal trainer.

Life is a tougher experience for some than it is for others. Tough times build muscles and make you stronger. The experiences that one will face serve to either make you (if the lessons are learned) or break you (if the lessons are ignored). No one is protected from the challenges that life will present. However, the effects will be lessened when wisdom is applied. It may be a good idea to use other people's situations as lessons to guide us. Parents try to convince their children not to make the same mistakes they made. It is natural for one to guard their offspring from the difficulties that they faced. They display strength and hide their vulnerability. But they often use that strength to create easier times for their children, so their muscles are underdeveloped. Easy times may seem attractive, but it encourages weakness. Learning how to get past tough times is a critical survival skill. If these skills are not developed, one will keep repeating the course until the lesson is learned.

LIFE LESSONS PT 30

Faith is a muscle...exercise it or lose it!

"Now faith is the substance of things hoped for, the evidence of things not seen." (Hebrew 11:1, KJV). The Bible gives numerous practical examples of the positive effects of faith. One of the key interpretations of faith is belief. Belief is confidence. Confidence can only be achieved through practice. If I say I believe in myself, but I display behaviors that does not match, then I am lying to myself. I must know that I "CAN." The Bible also states, "But wilt thou know, O vain man, that faith without works is dead?" (James 2:26, KJV). One does not walk around merely believing in themselves and not do anything with it. So, I must display my "CAN DO" attitude. I must use my talents if I am to achieve success. I must do the actions to prove that I believe in myself and my abilities. Faith, although credible, has some mysterious components. Faith produces results that sometimes cannot be explained through the natural lens. It is almost supernatural. As a praying woman, I have witnessed the effects of exercising my faith. I had a difficult pregnancy and had been advised by medical experts that abortion would be my best option when my liver enzymes were elevated. My stubborn nature coupled with my faith allowed me to stand up to a medical system that relied solely on science. I knew that although I trusted them, they did not have it all right. So, my days in the hospital were filled with coaxing with the hope that I would agree to terminate my pregnancy. I told them to try all the other options they had, but abortion is not on the table. Then I conversed with the Almighty. After six days, they discharged me with normal liver enzymes. Sometimes we give up too easily without exploring all the options. The moment an obstacle rolls in front of us, we panic and play dead. The answer is always there. We just do not see it.

Life Lessons Pt 31

If you plant a garden of thorns, butterflies will disappear. But if you build a beautiful garden they will live there.

Happiness is desired but it is not automatic. It is free, but not guaranteed. It is so simple that it is often overlooked. You must be intentional in finding it. And only you have the formula. Happiness is not about having everything you desire. It is being grateful for everything you have.

Mama Sylvie's last words to me were "If you cannot do good, don't do anything." If you present yourself to others as unhappy and disagreeable, they will avoid being around you for fear of you rubbing off on them. If you create an environment where others can thrive, they will be naturally drawn to you. Whatever one's desires, they must give what they want to get. You cannot give what you do not have. If you give away what is not yours then you are a thief. If you are empty, you cannot pour into others. If you do not know how to love, you cannot show someone love.

You attract what you are. When you smile at life, life smiles back at you.

Life Lessons Pt 32

You may be too much or not enough for someone. But you are just enough for the right person.

Our humanness yearns for companionship. The full value of joy comes when you share it with someone. So, we search for avenues to fit in. Be it a work or personal situation, we build relationships that satisfy a need(s). Everyone has their individual experiences that determine their expectations and how they treat with the world around them. Here in lies the problem. You may not always fit in their expectations, nor will they always fit into yours. This can be devastating to some. Unrealized expectations always hurt more than an open wound. The "fit" may come easier for others than it does for you, but that does not mean that you are doomed. If you do not love who you are when you are with someone then do not stay. There is someone for everyone. One who will accept all your flaws, craziness, joyfulness, and everything about you. Your person is out there. A compromise with a situation that takes away your peace is not worth it. Strengthen the person within and be confident that the "right" one will show up.

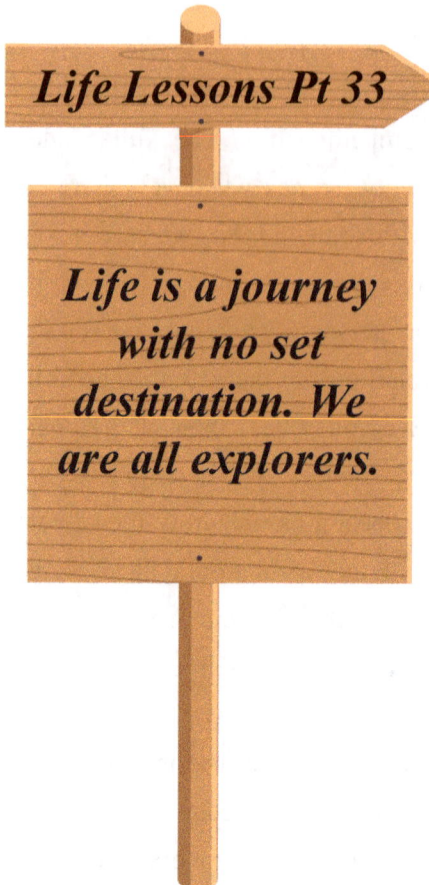

Life Lessons Pt 33

Life is a journey with no set destination. We are all explorers.

We all came in as a baby. A blank slate that life begins to write on the moment we are conceived. We walk this journey once, but if you do it right, once is enough!

You will not always have good days, but you can choose to face your bad days with different glasses on.

Do not let your destination distract you from celebrating the now or your small accomplishments.

Trust the journey, appreciate where you are, and learn from your missteps.

Live your life the way you want to leave your life. Your reputation will precede you.

The quicker you learn to laugh at yourself, the easier your life becomes. Life can be a beating stick if you take yourself too seriously.

You may have a rough path every now and again, but you have no idea what can come from your brokenness, if you give you broken pieces a chance to turn into newness of life.

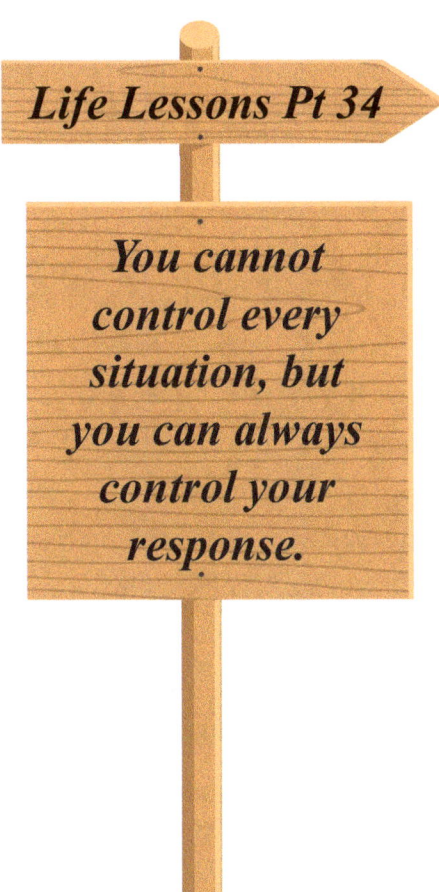

Life Lessons Pt 34

You cannot control every situation, but you can always control your response.

Negativity is all around us everywhere, every day. You cannot stop it from being out there, but you have the power to prevent it from finding a home in your life. It starts with the self. When you understand who you are, you will not just do or say anything. Self-control is strength. But it does not come easily. It takes a deep knowing of self to see through situations and give oneself the clarity required to formulate a response, or no response. Not everyone is meant to know your next move. Sometimes sitting still and remaining silent is your best move. It is said that a silent river runs deep. It has a calmness that few understands. And they may never be able to figure it out because they do not have enough information to make a judgment. Do not allow others to prompt or adjust your response at their will. You will always be their slave.

Life Lessons Pt 35

Vulnerability is not a weakness, it is strength.

Emotions come in assorted colors. They spice up life. They cannot be avoided. But they are often hidden. Boys are taught that they should not cry because it shows weakness. Women learn that if they are to be seen as capable in the workplace, they need to be "tough." Then all authenticity is lost in the quest to be "strong." Vulnerability may be misunderstood as weakness because it opens you to being physically and emotionally hurt. But it is those expressions that allow people to know that you are hurt. It is when one allows those wounds to embitter their progress that vulnerability is dangerous. I should be able to express myself without fear of being victimized. I should be able to show the colors that make me beautiful. I should be able to be ME. Being vulnerable builds trust and authenticity. Be mindful of that and learn how and when to blend them to make life beautiful.

Life Lessons Pt 36

If the world was filled with just blind people, who would you impress?

If money, titles, and degrees impress you, then you will be like a cow following cane band to the pound. The most genuine people will not flaunt their accomplishments. They pay it forward! The most beautiful people you will ever meet do not always grab your attention and they may not have any titles. But you must commit time to find them. They are usually diamonds in the rough. When people are stripped of their material clothes, they are just people, with no other choice but to be human. Recognizing their "sameness," that they alone cannot stand, that together, life is better, that the concept of better is an illusion they bought into. So, instead of allowing the narrative to dictate how we define ourselves and others, seek to be human first!

Life Lessons Pt 37

If you throw a stone into a crowd, you may not know who you hit, but that person will not forget he got hit.

When you hurt people, you do not always remember. But the one you hurt will not ever forget how you made them feel. We use words loosely without any concern for who we hurt. We do whatever makes us happy, even when it is at someone else's expense. No one should be so guarded of another's baggage that they cage their free expression. However, if it makes you feel good to put someone down, then you are the one with issues. It does not take a major act of physical strength to be the light in someone's day. Choosing what and when to say something is a testament of control. And that does not make you weak. It is in fact mastery of oneself.

Words are keys to open and close doors. Choose them wisely!

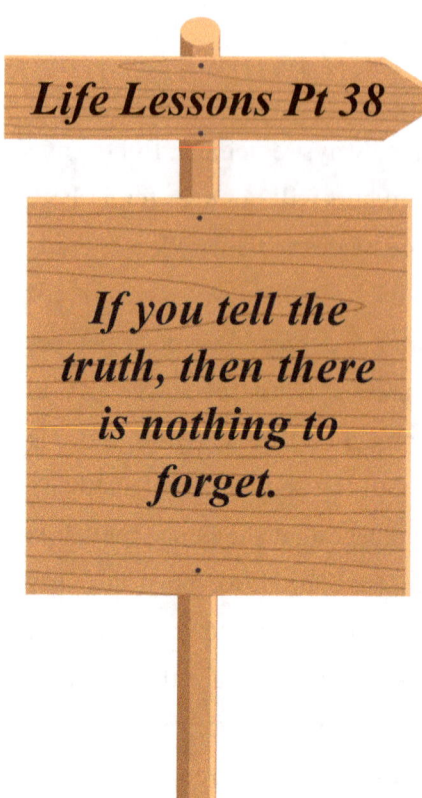

Life Lessons Pt 38

If you tell the truth, then there is nothing to forget.

I've been told that great liars also have the best memories. The first lie requires a follow up lie, until a web of deceit is woven. Perceiving that the "thing" that is desired won't be achieved will allow people to do strange things. I have seen people lie for reasons I could not understand. The truth may hurt deeply, but it is the truth. Although some will prefer the shield of a lie, the truth will hurt in one episode. Lies hurt in endless series.

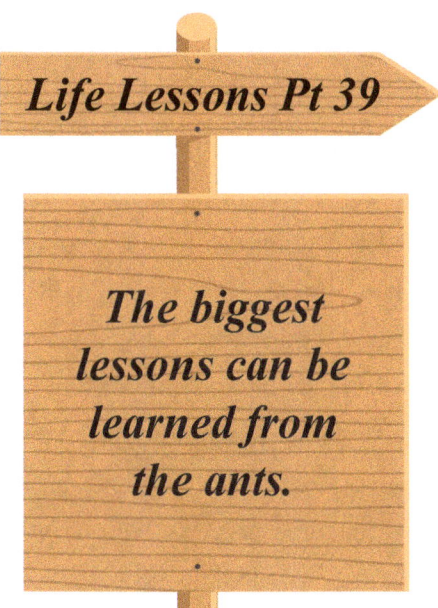

Life Lessons Pt 39

The biggest lessons can be learned from the ants.

Be careful whose advice or criticism you take. They may not be able to offer that service since they have not experienced what you have, or they don't have the capacity to understand your path. They can only advise you based on their knowing. You may have long exceeded theirs. There are however some invaluable lessons to be learned from the ants.

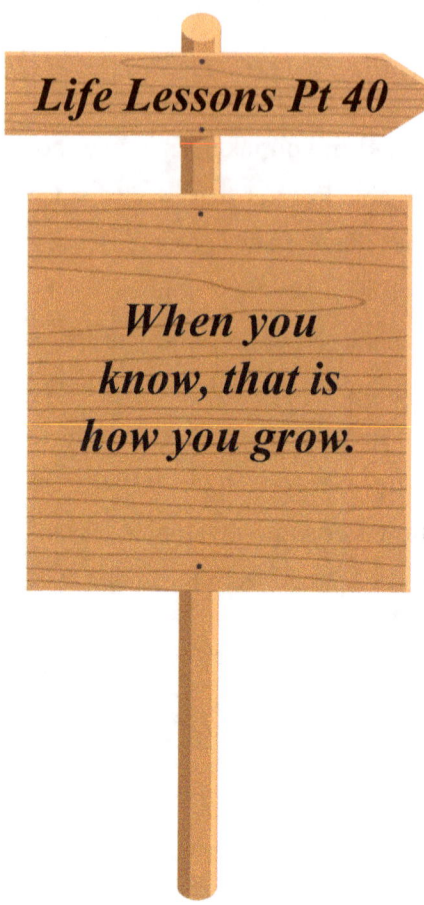

Life Lessons Pt 40

When you know, that is how you grow.

Knowing is to understand as truth, to experience, and to be familiar with. But this understanding will only come when there is intentionality around its discovery. If you want to have discipline in your life, do something every day that you hate doing. Then everything else will become painless. The monk can perform what seems like physically impossible maneuvers because he prepared himself by stretching what is usually deems as normal limits. He also used the power of the mind to bend his reality. Every answer to every question that you will ever have about yourself is inside of you. You just do not know it yet.

Be fearless, stand tall, be brave and let courage lead your journey. Be inquisitive without the drama. Question boldly the things you do not understand. It takes courage to be exceptional.

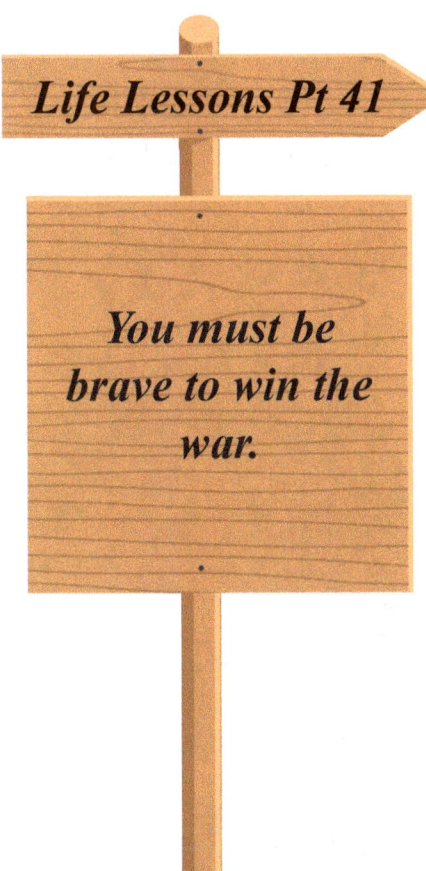

Life Lessons Pt 41

You must be brave to win the war.

Courage is not non-existence of fear, but the understanding of fear. You will have uncertainties, but you make your move anyway. You will have doubts, but it does not stand in your path like the great wall of China. And when the naysayers try to ambush you, you will prove them wrong. That is what a courageous spirit will do for you. It is there as a small voice that cheers you on and shows you the possibilities. It is the voice that you cannot allow to go silent. It cannot be brushed aside in the face of mountainous opposition. But you must know what the fight is about to fight.

LIFE LESSONS PT 42

Persistence is the intellect of achievement.

The river's path leads to the sea. It must get to the sea, by any means necessary. It will cut through a rock, not because of its power, but because of its persistence. It will break through a dam so it can flow. That is the power of persistence. It is the force that drives an action even when the reason is no longer apparent. It is the brains of achievement. Without persistence, the dream dies. Sometimes it is necessary to pause, rest, then resume. Give yourself grace. Enjoy the journey. Keep going!

Life Lessons Pt 43

The soil is the farmer's best tool.

The plant that is placed in the wrong soil or a pot that isn't big enough won't flourish. But if it is transplanted in the ideal environment it will thrive beyond your wildest imagination. The hypothetical soil can represent any aspect of your life. As a leader, I have had the opportunity to mold talent that were once considered dead. Giving attention to the little things, may lead to discovery of big things. People want to be seen, heard, and understood. Responding to them in a way that sparks their wick and continuously fueling them will allow their lights to shine brilliantly. We all have different talents. Finding the best soil to plant the seed in will produce a great crop! Has someone or something ever sparked a fire in you? Do you remember how you felt? Do you remember the things you did, the stops you pull out, the out of the box ideas you had and your drive to make them happen? That same energy is still inside you. That same drive is just lying there sleeping. Now that it is awake, use it!

Life Lessons Pt 44

You are my mirror!

I love you, lost you, mourned you, then moved on from you. Thanks for showing me the things I should not accept from others. I can now love you from a distance.

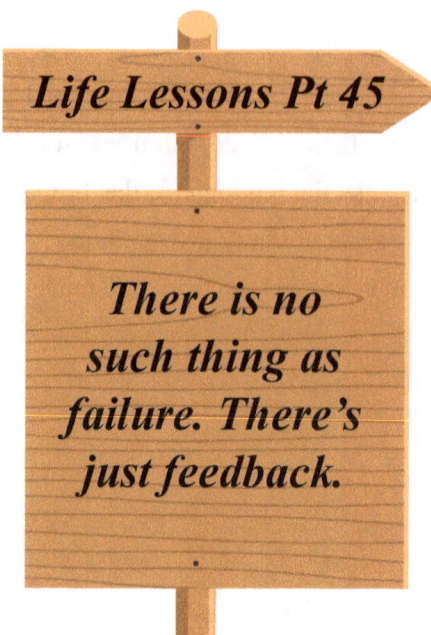

Life Lessons Pt 45

There is no such thing as failure. There's just feedback.

We often feel like we have failed when things did not go as planned. The effects can be devastating. Look for the gift within your problem. You will learn what does not work. But if you do not pay attention, you'll never stop getting feedback. You will continue to bump into walls repeatedly until you realize that you are the wall. Then the path will become clear.

Learn the lessons, pick yourself up, and keep the dream alive. There is no expiration date on dreams. You are still alive. It is never too late to make them happen.

Life Lessons Pt 46

Trust the process.

The plant grows from a seed to a plant. Then when it is mature enough it blossoms. Blossoms turn into fruits and the fruits develop into that thing you love. There is a period of bearing, harvest, and then rest. At some point that tree give up the ghost. Life cycles in their own seasons. The grape goes through the pressing and beating before it is aged to turn into fine wine. Your pressing and beating are to refine you and get you ready for your next chapter. Learn the lessons that life is teaching you. If you refuse to extract the lessons, you will never move through to the next stage. Do not get stuck… push yourself past the challenging times…there is a light at the end of the tunnel. There is a beautiful garden waiting on the other side.

Life Lessons Pt 47

Boxes should only be used for packages.

Do not lock yourself in a box with titles. Your gifts are many. Explore them and keep redefining yourself.

Life Lessons Pt 48

Everyone has a chapter they do not want anyone to read.

As we write the chapters of our life, be mindful of the highlights and the low points. Make the highlights count and be intentional about reducing the low points. Be who you say you are and be proud of the you that you strive to become. Treat people as good as you are. Do not stoop down to their level. Remember life is a journey. A journey comes with disappointments, joys, surprises, impressive moments, and rough tides. But there are lessons to be learned and experiences to enjoy. You have one life, it is up to you to make it great.

Life Lessons Pt 49

Time waits for no man.

Time moves with or without you. If you decide to forget that principle you only hurt you. For something to be precious it must be in limited supply. Time is one such thing. Treasure it with everything you have. It is irreplaceable.

So

Love and be loved.

Dream big and action them!

Learn all you can about everything you can!

Do what you love every chance you get!

Believe in yourself more than anyone else can!

Pray, it brings you closer to The Almighty!

Above all, make every moment your best moment!

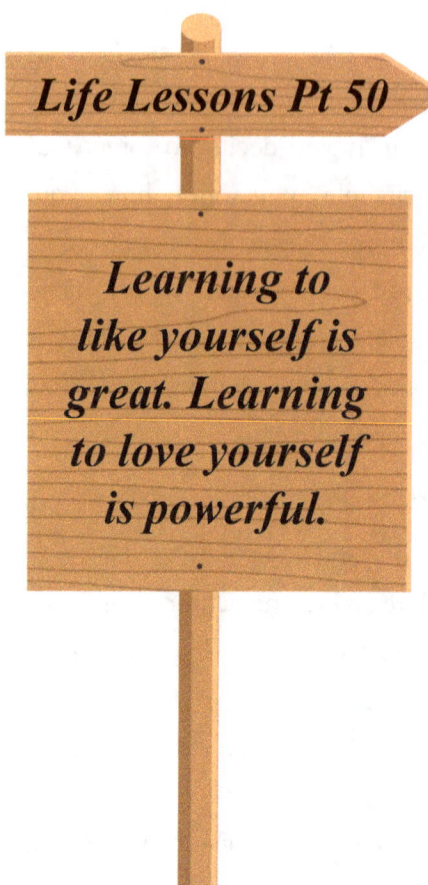

Life Lessons Pt 50

Learning to like yourself is great. Learning to love yourself is powerful.

The most challenging job you will ever have is to work on yourself. But it is the most rewarding.

People will never rise above the opinion of themselves. So, strive to always have a healthy one:

Do not compare yourself with others. You will always be unhappy. Try being a better version of yourself every day.

Do yourself a favor. Watch what you speak and guard what you hear. Your ears are a gateway to your peace.

Never use your tongue to curse myself.

Make peace with your past so it does not control your present and future. It has already done and cannot be undone. Do not give it power over you. Rivers never flow backwards. It does not matter how rough the tide. Getting through the rough times may look impossible but you must move forward like the river. The past should not hold you back. Reflect on it and let it motivate you to push ahead. Stay focused on the bright future that you have ahead.

Stop throwing a pity party. You are all you got. The sooner you realize that the better your life will become. Forgiveness is the single most important thing you can do for yourself. It purges your blood.

Run Your Race

When life's challenges come knocking
Threatening to slow your pace
Brace your back against the wind
And let it propel your ship
The waters may get muddy
But you must never stall
Though the path isn't clear
You must run your race

When the rain begins to fall
And the eminent floods rage
Those grim moments are thinking times
Meant to be seen as prime
Keep the momentum going strong
And dust the dirt that formed
Face your nerves and bring it along
Tell it we must run this race

Hope may be a distant friend
But its outstretched hands hang still
Reach out farther than you've ever been
There's more to you than your best
Put your strength to the test
You'll surprise you and the rest
No matter what you do

You must run your race
When you get to the final stretch
And the finish line is in sight
Regrets are folks you shouldn't meet
Leave them standing along the side
Time is the master but when it wanes
No more you can recall
Trust your gut and cross the line
And finish your race with pride

I'm Growing

I've broken through the seed of discord
Into a cold world where storms are still the norm
In search of a higher height at which I can see
And rise above the surface teething pains

I've appreciated the ground beneath
To nurture my roots and keep me warm
In hope that when hurricanes pass
They'll hold me firmly as long as it last

I've seen other buds beside me grow
I call them friends but they may be foes
Fighting for the same dream I whispered in their ears
Because they didn't know theirs was waiting in this sphere

I sometimes break a limb
Feels like I'm stumbling uphill
Every inch that I achieve
Is challenged by the higher wind speed

I've learned that ebb and flow
Is the perfect rhythm of life
For the pull that feels like pain
Is the push for me to gain

Now I hold power in this clasp fist
Not to wield it when I feel like throwing a fit
But to breath and walk away
So, I can live to fight another day

For every lesson that's been taught
Is strength to overcome past battles fought
And never succumb to hatred's call
Cause now I'm standing strong and tall

TEMPORARY TRAVELERS

Along the riverbanks of time
Stood an old bridge that has lost its shine
Its rustic rails stained with grime
Collected from the ruins of slow decline
But the memories she holds are unrefined
Left by failing hearts that were once prime
So, she sits under the big holm oak tree
Listening to the hum of the river beneath her feet

She often journeys within to reminisce
The first day she bridged the wedge of prejudice
For though the waters of misconception flowed deep
No one dear to brave the social tides that they'll reap
So, she stretched across the banks of opposing sides
Arching the floods between her thighs
With Dahomey strength she held them tight
To calm unreasonable fears that caused their fight

When the tsunamis of life lift its unforgiving veil
And drains their blood making them pale
The medicine in between her curative rails
Will pour like water into their empty pails
But the gifts she gives to the most frail
Lies in the silent places of their malicious tale
For the moments not spent on self-blackmail
Will slowly usher in the sweet gale

Take your time to slither past the welcome mat
Even when you're endlessly dragged by your sorrowful chat
Look beneath her rugged terrain for a reflection staring back
And let the suffering flow wherever the timeless rivers go
Sometimes the pain is embedded deeper than you know
Desperately holding to your glow
But the deafening silence will steal the show
For on the other end of sadness beautiful flowers grow

Then at the end of her life she sits agaze
Missing the floods of emotional craze
Refusing to enjoy her quiet laze
For the chasm in time has left her lost in this lonely maze
As she sheds the light of her last phase
Her final request is to remain grounded in this old sway
In memory of service to those who lost their way
And temporary travelers whose home was just one decision away

FOOLS FAIRYTALE

When meandering through this journey of ice and gold
Hoping that the end will be when you're old
Scaling the paths that makes you tired or bold
You'll realize it's a fairytale in a fool's world

When it feels like it has no rhyme or reason
Never trick yourself into committing treason
Or fight the battles to satisfy your ego
For only self is sovereign in any season

The greatest teacher one can find
Are the mistakes we leave behind
Granted you extracted truths from lessons taught
So, when it repeats you won't be so distraught

There are many paths of access
Some may come without a recess
But if you seek clarity before you get yourself in a mess
Then you'll save yourself a world of stress

This game of fools is amazingly beautiful
When you learn the rules to being bountiful
Though it's filled with infinite obstacles
It's also an interesting bag of possibilities

PEOPLE LIKE ME

People like me are that tree
By the river's edge
Hidden beneath the murky mud lines
Deep within its lowest reaches
With uncovered existence that seem completely starved
Rooted in the rubble of suitable soil
Staring at the periphery that houses passersby
On the banks of this old narrow dirt track

People like me respects life's winds
Knowing that she'll always be a passing friend
Sometimes in a soft embrace
Other time she leaves without a trace
She'll break the branches that extends
Or merely sheds the leaves
But when her wrath is quenched
She'll cool the raw wounds

People like me have sinuous paths
Rare supple and gracefully intricate
When it rains, I dance with the drops of chance
When it's cold I bow to preserve my heart
If it's warm outside then it's cool inside
But I always watch the river's strides
As it meanders along for a usual ride
And finally, to greet at estuary's side

People like me are in sync with time
Connected to the divine
And understands that there's purpose in being alive
For with weathering the storms and tides
There's strength to be found in the mud
But when that strength wanes
And it seems like it defeats the gains
They'll remember

BOWL OF TRUTH

Here are a few truths I hold dear
Within my grasp they're always near
These irrefutable friends I'll defend without fear
When volatile attacks try to smear

When strength is tested on winter's icy hills
And the darkest days are at a standstill
I brace my back against the wind
Even if it feels like an endless drill

There's courage deep inside
Within my spirit it resides
Reach farther than I've ever been
Awakening the bravest me within

When love knocks at my door
It should mirror everything I have in store
For my first love should be me
Then what's inside will come shining through

Dream the dreams that children do
Unrestricted, colorful, and true
Purge the lies that cover your eyes
To let loose creativity from its disguise

The lion's roar they'll all respect
In his domain he's king at best
Never question your power within
Believe you can run like the wind

The acrid smoke from life's ashy path
Will stick and fester causing pure wrath
But if small as a mustard seed
Faith sees a way and it will lead

I hope in me the sun will rise
And brighten the darkness on the inside
This bowl of truth is all I have
To weather the storms of this strange land

MISUNDERSTOOD

There's a value that's placed on everything
Weak minds even give their lives for common things
The biggest problem we often face
Is to slow our pace to fit others race

I hold my peace above all else
Hoping your respect will recognize
That boundaries are not walls
But doors that can invite you in

I've been stripped naked in a crowd
Wrapped in bondage and my inside screams aloud
Chained to a galloping horse and a plow
But now this resilient being stands proud

Now that I choose to breathe again
With all spiritual graffiti I'll contend
One foot in front of the other
Taking back my infinite power

I won't shrink to fit your frame
Neither be engulfed in your fiery flame
Here is my temple of truth
I live happily even if misunderstood

JOURNEY TO SELF

There are still several stories to tell
Many chapters written
Several more to come before the book ends
No edits to be done
For those were written well
Cause journeys are made of planes valleys and variations of hilltops

There are many bridges to be burnt
And several left to cross
Not every pathway was meant to get you across
The ones that break weren't meant to last
While others will crack
But endure long enough for you to pass

With different species you must cohabitate
Even when envy will cause them to hate
Some will pretend to show you love that's great
To serve themselves and distract you from the race
Don't miss red flags along the way
But package them well for the shelf on which they'll stay

Don't be quick to criticize the mirror
Believe what you see before you face sorrow
Change is constant
It flows like the sea

There's many a slip between the cup and the lip
So, make room for you to heal and grow

The flow of the tide may break your sails
Life's winds may gust and make you frail
Shallow heights may seem impossible to scale
But if you lose sight of the sweet gale
The stripes you've earned will only be pale

Only few will finish this journey to self
For those who do
Many secrets they'll tell
To soften the blows and save you from hell
Your greatest enemy is yourself
But only you can take this journey to self

DO OVER

Let the mistakes of yesterday
Be lessons for today
The darkness seen along the way
Should brighten someone else's day
What good it does if what you did
Was just another play
When on that stage
Your grandeur displays
Was only for the show

Life often gives us unmerited grace
Even when not deserved
To reflect review and revive anew
The things that sometimes hurt
Renewed enthusiasm and a fresh start
May have you feeling smart
Lost success may be a mess
But don't you stress
Do over is a new test

Inner muscles are often built
On life's roughest roads
Emotional grit is on the list
When there's no option to fail
For the road to success

May be filled with hard tests
But the skill to win is within
Find that new gear
And hold on my dear
The second time may be a charm

Don't compare yourself to anyone else
For there was only one you
The only aim is to win that game
Between the best versions of you
To have perfection
Is not a part of the plan
But there are some that do
You could be 1 or 98 we still make mistakes
A do over will keep us straight

LONELY TREE

When life's raging winds begin to blow
And round about you splinters your soul
Don't give up now or put on a show
You are closer to the prize than you know

The support you seek you cannot find
In times of need you are left behind
The tree that's alone on the distant land
Bear deeper roots than those other ones

Though pastel hues and subdued shade
Hides your delicate beauty which may appear fade
The courage to stand alone and live
Is certainly farther than skin deep

Your solitary existence does not confine
No obstacles around your roots to bind
Beneath your earth treasures you'll find
Rugged beauty of infinite girth

Take your time to weather the storms
Learn the lessons deep within
One day soon your own forest you'll create
To lend your strength to other lonely trees

ASHES ARISE

From the ash of defeat, you'll rise to meet newness of life
Leaving behind every fragment of your unforgiving fight
The skies will whisper your name with bountiful delight
These ashes lay lifeless yet your new being arise

The beauty from above is unparalleled at best
Introduce yourself and worry not about the rest
Take the flight of faith put yourself to the test
These chains couldn't hold you so freely step out from the nest

When the arduous winters round about you wail
And steep mountains in the distance seem impossible to scale
Look at your inward being and tell it to prevail
From the ashes of your torment, you'll smell the sweet gale

LIVE NOW

I'm nervous about my tomorrows
When I think of all my past sorrows
Robs me of my peace today
And my mind wanders around all day

I'm sorry for the mistakes I made
Though the lessons from them I've learned
The familiarity of failure and pain
Cripples my present gains

I'm angry with people who's done me wrong
My emotions are weak but my body is strong
The mask I wear around while singing a song
Shields fragility so I can cruise along

I'm scared today to open my eyes
Things I may see would tear apart my disguise
This I must do so my soul can rise
Live in the present allow peace to be a surprise

Nature's Best

Of all the things I've seen
And all the places I've been
To witness talented displays and scenes
None can compare to nature's delight

The greatest joy it can ever bring
Is to watch a new day like clockwork ring
As light pushes the darkness aside
It's attachments all around will sing

Blue hues embrace the clouds in the sky
Bending low to kiss the ocean's floor
The distance not enough to disrupt their love
Leaving space in between for you and I

The rugged beauty of the seashores
Hugs the mountains' feet a little more
Every time it's waters massage it to its core
Majestic hallelujahs crash loud like a roar

Floating around are dreams to dream
Mystical rhythms or so they seem
But we are the music makers waiting to beam
If we dare to take that leap though it may produce some steam

Nature's best will put your mind to the test
Cause It will never take a beauty rest
In all its spender and glory best
Fill your heart that's sometimes a mess

Take time daily to savor its view
Approach it gently like you're in the pew
Let your feet caress the morning dew
It will thank you for being one of the few

Courage To Live

Have you scratched the surface
Of the courage hill
Cast your whims
That around you swim
Shake the ripened fruit from low hanging limbs
Dig in repeatedly its power will never trim

Believe Life holds such promise
Good or bad depends on your premise
Refuse to break your embrace from this journey
Even when it seems life's a burden

If you think of yourself as meek
Don't be surprised when you're perceived as weak
Inner strength shouldn't always wear like a sleeve
But show up in moments when you most need

Life's first glimpse none can recall
Limitless beauty awaits though pain will stall
Through varying degrees of intimacy with one and all
It's Conveyor belt continues to crawl

The wide-eyed giant called experience stares
Saddle less blows it throws and kicks like mares
Minimize its effect no don't you dare
Impressive arsenals you must wear

Life's flavor may lack licorice root
But look forward to having a sweet tooth
When moments bring on the deep-sea blues
Embrace it full with the courage to live!

BEFORE YOU LET GO

Before you let go take time away from your stress
Bring to the forefront the memories that are best
Don't hold back the laughter and happy tears
Embrace the feeling when life returns to your breast

Before you let go recall the dreams you once dreamt
Whisper secrets only to the universe you'll tell
Savor the fire that will build in your well
Leave a little space for oxygen so that fire won't quell

Before you let go take a 360-degree view
Observe God's creation in their seasons anew
The thorn is watered for the sake of the rose
Remember you are one of his creations too

If you must let go know that I will miss you
Cause there was none quite as unique as you
Relearning to walk can be a painful process
But I'll hold your hand to support every step

MOMENTS IN TIME

Only one moment is given at a time
Choose well how you spend each dime
Worry and happiness occupy the same space
Use them well before they disappear

What good does it do to break your back
Carrying heavy burdens around like a back pack
A positive outlook will certainly lighten your load
Push away wrinkles gray hairs and lessen your pain

For the sake of the rose thorns are watered too
Rain won't select the melon and not the honey dew
Life trials stresses but it will strengthen you
Don't pull over in the storm you have to drive all the way through

Moments in time will never return
When they pass by it's yours to discern
Life is made of good bad and ugly
What's past is finished so enjoy the present

LIVE FULL

Like a tree Dreams are left floating in the wind
Waiting for you to snatch them limb by limb
Deeply rooted in possibilities for those who will
Dare to climb the perennial trunk of time

The innocence of childhood attracts its glow
An intimate dance that will put on a show
Left unattended it's potential you'll never know
Fill the blank slates and watch them grow

The world you leave without a trace
Will miss your fire to light many pathways
Only you can give life to your dreams
Live life full so death will have nothing to steal

WHEN MOTHERS DIE

When mothers die good children go through the pit of hell
But God has His secrets that only He alone can tell
And so far, He has chosen to keep those secrets well
But He loaned us mothers and now He must retrieve His angel

Like a worm in a bud, we're fed by her womb
Nine months of discomfort some even made it to the tomb
A labor of love she endured amidst her gloom
God's hands formed you though she never jumped over the broom

She's done her part and brought you thus far
Like a magician she creates something out of nothing without a war
Her top priority is preventing your scar
Only God in His wisdom could have left that door ajar

Now it's time her crown she must wear
Don't be shy if you must shed a tear
She prepared you well to find your next gear
Though your heart and soul is left bare

Hang on to Him for dear life and comfort my dear
For that's all you can ever do
Smile your smile even as you are hurting
Because believe me, you are one of His angels too

FALLING UP

Have you ever taken that leap of faith?
How about that fall from grace into that place and space that's
perfectly positioned to cushion your mission
Who said you couldn't defy gravity though you know the of brevity
of your existence
Spread your wings and feel the wind massage your under belly
Measure the immeasurable flight from fall of fail to falling up

Don't look down at the what was
Ignoring the mystery
Don't take for granted your history
But taste and see the ALL-POWERFUL ONE'S chemistry

I know you didn't see me coming
LikeMaya I'm hot air I rise
Light like a feather but
Solid as a rock

I know you never imagined
That my breast didn't touch the ground
My prowess wouldn't be dumbed down
And you would dumbfound

Hey you…yes YOU!
Falling up is a skill that's acquired

When you stay on your knees in prayers
Talking on and on like you're wired
And not fearing the eyes and the liars

So, face your fear and whims
Speak to your arms and limbs
Bet your foes and kins
Flee your chains and links
Muster your strength and
Step off those pins
If you're going to fall....
Fall UP!

THAT THING CALLED LIFE

As the mystery unfolds about this thing called life
Realities for many cuts deep like a knife
With every day received a chance and a choice
And subliminal messages programmed without a fight
What do we know about this thing called life?

Examples of those before well lived or sometimes trite
Should provide directions for good or bad they might
Prevent headaches heartaches or plight
But only fools cut off their nose just for spite
Is there a right way for this thing called life?

Could there be a switch for some to have delight
And other to only experience darkness in the light
There's no rewind or erase for what you write
But What if in one's control there's a night
When all could change to everything bright
Would that be your idea of a perfect life?

From birth to death our little dash we write
With All encounters you can exercise your choice
And restart tomorrow morning with a prayer and a chance
If your little dash extends beyond your trance
Grab the bull by the horn belong to the present
Life is way too short to waste its presence.

FLOAT ON

The long winding seas across villages and towns
Leads to the footpath of life's greatest hills
A glance at the top creates an uneasy thrill
But there's no flowing backwards the momentum must build

When the tides of emotions wash high against the grain
And the adrenaline rush violently about your brain
Look forward to the possibilities that will calm the raging seas
Then paddle slowly over waters that lead to unimaginable glee

If the oceans seem filled with various rivers flowing in
It awaits your stream of life to balance its waters deep
Let your flavor stir newness to rejuvenate palates on repeat
Create colors to paint the midnight sky

PRAY WITHOUT CEASING

Rejoice in the spirit always
Give thanks to your eternal guide anyway
Despite of circumstances we face these days
The breath you breathe is not withheld today

When misery chases the edge of your heel
And the soul screams from wounds that won't heal
Whisper a quiet prayer into the atmosphere
Prayer without ceasing will draw God near

If dark spirits fight to block your path
And your response is to pour out all your wrath Quiet prayers
sanctifies the atmosphere
Then watch roadblocks disappear into thin air

Joy and gratitude will come your way
Even when words you cannot say
Whisper quiet prayers in your happy times
Praying without ceasing will elevate your incline

THE WILL

Tomorrow we'll never see
It's an escape from current reality
All present moments must be
Lived in fullness of clarity
For when the moments pass
The weight of regret will forever last
Then the shadow that it cast
Covers the path that should be crossed

When things are left undone
And your best light is outshone
The victories that could be won
Are now defeated one by one
Unhinge the cords that bind
Your will is not one that is blind
For it is there to fuel your grind
Even when you're struck in the tide

Prayer and Praise

Take me to that place where I can rest
That place where all the broken pieces will reconnect
Give me the strength to swim through all the putrid mess
And help me to release all this pain and stress

Take me to the place where I can see my hidden self
Be the mirror that reflects the one who's stealth
And when the light falls on my darkened place
Help me never to retreat from grace

Take me higher than the distant sky
Release my wings so I can fly
And when I finally meet my tribe
Teach me to embrace them with joy and pride

Take me to my forever home
So, I may never be alone
When the day closes its eyes
I will rest on white clouds on high

ALIVE

Like the blossom of flowers in the dawn of spring
And the dew of autumn mornings gently touching my skin
As the melodic hum of the forest in my ear ring
My spirit dances to every rhythm and tune they sing

In moments of silence the humble heart hears
The voices of childlike beauty whispering in their ears
Though the mutterings are indistinct it calms all fears
When the noise of life quiets then unspeakable peace appears

It's not just the rise and fall of the air we breathe
Or the lived experiences that make us believe
But when the unexpected gift of laughter comes when pain won't
leave
Then calming waters flow to resurrect and conceive

Though life doesn't always give beauty for ash
Or the turbulent tides all around you wash
Sit with the flow don't force the currents
The dark and the light must run concurrently

LOOKING BACK

I travel down the winding streets with fear
Over the smooth rocks and those as sharp as spears
Meandering through a path that was once clear
Just to get lost in the ocean of despair

I carry along all the memories of my past
Even those that tremble at my wrath
Though I'm a hostage to the doubts I cast
It cannot save me from the ocean so vast

I long for the ocean to disappear
For it swallows all the memories I hold dear
But I must risk losing the narrow comforts of fear
To have the abundant hand of the ocean appear

So, I travel with my best rhythm to the edge of the sea
From the ashes of my fears, I frolic with pure glee
No more looking back on what no longer serves me
The ocean awaits to fill the empty spaces

THE PERFECT VOICE

Deep on the inside of you
Lies something that's dying to come through
Gently parting the rigid brush
Fighting to escape the indescribable crush

It may scream aloud
At a time when you're not proud
Or it sometimes merely whispers
The little warnings of things sinister

It may start with just a tiny tap
Then a thump on the soft spot in your back
But if you listen carefully when it speaks
It will guide you to your peak

It may not have a poet's style
Or create the world's most famous lines
But its message is always crystal clear
Even when your heart is a little scared

We all have that perfect voice
Some may choose to compromise
Never ignore the greatest teacher
Alway trust your inner self

I HAVE SEEN HEAVEN

The heaven that is beyond the sky
And the mystical underworld hidden from you and I
Where departed souls divide and meet
Up on high well lived lives will greet
Missed opportunities on earth they leave
For a place they'll never see

Good and Evil are identical twins
Vanquished fears and trampled whims
None can deny these truths in themselves
When despite pleas and prayer requests
Can't dismiss one side and honor the best
For the slaver's heart won't let them rest

Finally, the clutter in your head will clear
Misery released your tired soul from its snare
Though in blood-soaked rags you appear
An escapee from this murderous affair
Now the clamor of birds sings in your ear
And peace resonates beyond compare

When you shall find that one moment in time
When your dreams and your realities align
In that blissful moment you will discover a life sublime
An inner place where no vicissitude can confine

Then the skies will be your ground
For you've walked the streets of heaven's highways

LOVE FREEDOM

I am yet to be revealed
Surrounded by skin and flesh
Grounded by sharp edged bones
And few elements I'll never know
This unique mind I possess
May seem to be a confusing mess
But I know that comes what may
I'm molded from the creator's clay

I disregard selfish Love that holds
Because it will never serve until it's old
For when there are trying times
It will pretend like it is blind
I Seek the love that liberates
One that will refuse to break
Heals the wounded with its lips
Mends the seams that once had rips

Liberated love is pure and free
Will hold no grudges against me
But in my weakened vulnerable state
Embraces me like a divine mate
Who is this bird that soars so high
Yet clasps its wings around lowly things
Its mystery will forever bring
A song that all would love to sing

Reflections

There's a bridge you must cross on your journey to self
And its waters are never knee deep
On both sides they'll stare when you look at yourself
But sometimes the picture isn't complete

The path may be lonely the silence is loud
For with you there will be no crowd
One step at a time one glimpse from behind
And reflections you cannot deny

The person that stares back you may not recognize
For time has made them a slave
Stare dead in the eyes don't be mesmerized
It is them that knows you best

The final test is to be true to yourself
For with you you're stuck clear to the end
Before you get pass take one last look at the start
Cause with that person you must make amends

EVERYONE

Everyone that comes along
Is part of a strategic plan
No matter how brief their moments
Rest assured they were meant to be

Everyone that comes along
May not be the one you love
They may be the only one who
Can love you through your mess

Everyone that comes along
Has a lesson to teach
Of compassion and caring endless sharing
Or to help you hold on to your self

Insurmountable obstacles will come
That is when you need someone
To show you a path to your strength
From deep inside your courage heap

So, when life throws you detours
Learn the lessons before
You move along your path
So, you don't experience life's wrath

YOUR LIGHT

I heard my name amidst the noise
Faintly traversing the midnight skies
Asking for your wick to be relit
To chase away darkness in the morning light

Everyone needs help along the way
Breath your cares into the air and pray
The right ears will be tuned just say
Doors will open amidst your dismay

Many wicks I've lit from this torch
Illuminate paths that's not quite as bright
Opening blind eyes to see great insight
Recalling strength to their delight

You did the work you exercised your faith
Giving you a chance to make a break
No repayment required today
Use your light to brighten someone's day

BE STILL

The illusion of time
Is like a thin line
Fragile but Impenetrable
Potent but Quiet
Agility undefined
A constant one-man dance
Though the music will cease
It will never be still

I sleep on its breast
Awake in its grasp
I travel alongside
It's unimaginable line
Moments are precious
Too pure to release
Though I clutch my chest
It slips from my grip
But I must be still

The richest among us can't buy it
If wishes would only come true
When life flashes before you
What good are your riches to you
Its value is realized in love
But hate we chose to do

Savor the little things that matter
It's those little things that's worth all the riches
The biggest bank account can never do

An oasis you'll find
When it's on your side
It builds mountains high
Leaves you on the decline
It will dictate your pace
If you stay in a gaze
Though you see the clock
Not one minute you can stop
Remember row your boat
To the beat of your own tune
Listen to its rhythm
Don't forget to be still

CREATOR

The abyss of time is like a thin line
That stands between nothingness and the great incline
Confusing many, others have even gone blind
Refusing to believe there's an Almighty who's divine

The myths appear to reflect their tricks
Big band theories slide stealthily off their lips
They say Ape evolution caused me to look this lit
So, from whence did apes come, isn't it mystic?

How much do you know about your maker?
Isn't He a master craftsman and a great baker?
For I am His product and I'm sure you want to be a taker
Yet you fail to give credit to the creator

In your head He placed His thoughts
Called them talents for with this you'll start
Building an empire then forward you must pass
Use them wisely and your legacy will last

Remove your blindfold Look around you and immense satisfaction
you'll find
When you listen to all of His creation combined
Birds, flowers, bees, symphonic and divine
All greatness is from Him, only the creator could have everything
aligned

THE LIGHT HOUSE

The final curtain calls
Chasing the darkness away
His eyes dimmed at the sight of the birds
Race towards the sunset place

As his favorite mug left his lips
Barely able to take his final sip
Eyelids fight their final war
watching sun and moonlight dance at dawn

75 years of priming the wick
Those before him a traditional gimmick
Nothing could prepare him for this unknown peace
As he sat at his final resting place

When grandparents take their final bow
One grandchild their secrets must know
The night light cannot cease to glow
Even when winter is thick with snow

Grief will challenge everything you learned
His legacy should not be wrapped up in that urn
Play the game like they're watching every turn
Keep the lighthouse lit and make them proud

THE PUNCHING BAG

The pendulum of life swings to and fro
Where it will rest no one knows
Listen to its rhythm and watch its flow
It will sometimes bring out your glow

If you approach it with wrath, it's weight will sting at the blow
It's not a fight but sometimes practice dipping your head low
For when courage has no sense of direction it will know
The teacher is your strength never sacrifice him to grow

The punching bag swings gently on its hinges
Those before you never left it like fringes
Contribute to the momentum for your touch matters
Absorb its energies and break forget the binging
Be intentional learn its secrets and mysteries

FEAR

It crippled my existence
Opened my eyes to the closed doors and closed my eyes to those that
were open
Illuminated inconsequential things and distracted me from what could
have been
It was a cryptic message re my awakening

If you refuse to unpack the thing that's possible
Cover your light and potential of which you are capable
You'll miss out on exploring all that God placed inside you
Then what a waste of a life that's so impeccable

What if there were no right way to do things right
What if you were misled into thinking about that plight
How then will you come up with what's your delight
If you refuse to deep dive into yourself beyond the night

A leap of faith they say will bring abundance
Chose to believe in the belief of independence
Of thought and innovation let new possibilities be your cadence
Once you kiss its sweet waters exercising prudence
The anxiety will transform everything in your existence

What if you could turn frantic behavior into fuel
Excuses into excellence

Anguish into ambition and
Resistance into resounding success
Then fear would be nothing but a healthy dose of necessity

HELL

I've experienced heaven in the midst of hell
Like no other there are several secrets to tell
When the fire inside refuses to quell
I bury it deep in this never ending well

When this raging inferno that I've been dealt
Pounds so hard against this back filled with welt
Threaten to swallow me whole so I'll melt
And stole everything besides my strength

Down broken roads I've been sent
Searching for parts of me in the darkened nightfall
With none but these shoulders on which I could fall
So, I turned within to answer that call

Somewhere deep in the abyss of time
There's a beautiful being standing in line
Waiting for you to see them as prime
Be one with them and forever you'll shine

The taste of pain will linger on your tongue
Emerging from smoke you'll be ready to run
Just like the moon rejuvenated and free
From the ashes of hell your heaven arises

I Told Myself

I told myself I wouldn't shed a tear
When out the door your love disappears
Disrupting my rhythm filling me with despair
I thought it prudent to pretend I didn't care

I told myself what's broken shouldn't be repaired
Find new ones to fill the gaping hole left in there
Then my heart pulls off the worst kind of scare
Refusing another this burden is too much to bear

I told myself that time will heal
Old wounds only scar they won't reveal
Pain and suffering are temporary it won't return
But the memories of love haunt and repeat

I told myself that love will cease
When the distance in between is wider than the seas
But yearnings lit the fire that warms my breast
Especially at nights when alone I rest

I told myself be strong don't weep
Even though your love I couldn't keep
I wished Love would return to the nest to sleep
So, I wouldn't rest in the bosom of defeat

Now I tell myself the simple truth
No more lies cause only me I fool
I'll keep loving you it can never cool
Even when my head wants to be stubborn and rule

PURPOSE

Don't listen to the noisemakers
Who want you to believe that there's no greatness in you
Tear you down and heap loads of stuff on you those are back breakers
Share no thoughts with them they are only naysayers
Find your purpose stay on track and focus there's greatness waiting to
come out

Look beyond what's in front of you
Stare deep into the distance too
Keep going and light you will see
Though dim at first and you may thirst
Along dry deserts sometimes lie an oasis
Find your purpose stay on track and focus there's greatness waiting to
come out

You may not be the first
Thinking that this is a curse
Doubting and self-sabotaging then immerse
Drowning In self-pity until you end up worst
That's the devil's plan
Find that gear and reverse
Find your purpose stay on track and focus there's greatness waiting to
come out

Uncover your light
Do it with all your might

Let it shine bright

Even if you have to toil late into the night

You'll find it feels right

With yourself you don't need to fight

Find your purpose stay on track and focus there's greatness waiting to

come out of you!

COME LORD

Lord, I want to be made whole
In the garden of Gethsemane I long to stroll
I crave your gentle touch of comfort untold
Come fetch me and bring me back to the fold

Lord I long to experience life anew
To thrive in your promise like the birds and the beasts too
Take away all of tomorrow's burdens I knew
So, my heart won't always feel this blue

Lord snatch me from this distant land
Give me hope and take me by the hand
With your strength I know I can stand
For with you I know there's a life that's grand

Lord speaks to my limbs so that they can move
Snatch me from this lame life and give me a rhythmic groove
Resurrect my dry bones and to me prove
That my baseless doubts of you I should remove

Lord helps me to see that still small light
Shower me with blessings with all of your might
I will be grateful and in me you will delight
Come now Lord and take away this fight

SECRET PLACE

If you look at you from outside yourself
Between you and yourself all secrets dwell
When the time is right it will begin to tell
Then foolish beliefs you will repel

There's an inner space to explore
Where there's everything and so much more
Strength wisdom and endurance galore
The truth in you it will restore

When you get lost in life's stream
Or you've been robbed of your dream
Follow the currents and you'll redeem
And your light will begin to gleam

Like a feather on water, you will be light
Let go of the strain and senseless fight
Set free your flow and clear your sight
Within yourself there's pure delight

When you meet the dark side of your soul
Never think that the good side it stole
For both were meant to be part of the same mold
Embrace both and melt into pure gold

When like all information seek
Some like wind and some to keep
Be your own mirror to reflect your grief
Let the waste water flow through your creek

ETERNITY

When the leaves lose their hue
And the flowers colors drain
Until the sun refuses to shine
And the rainbow hides its face
Even when there's no blue sky
Or a raindrop coming through
Remember, I'll always love you

When the challenges of life
Sits heavy on your chest
And it seems there's no light
At the tunnel's end at best
Look round about your breast
I'll be the embrace to calm your fears
Remember, I'll always love you

When the orchestra plays the final tune
And the distant music leaves
They'll be memories of me
Humming sweetly in your ear
If the birds refuse to sing
Let them take their rest my dear
Remember, till eternity, I'll always love you

www.ingramcontent.com/pod-product-compliance
Lightning Source LLC
Chambersburg PA
CBHW071151120626
46546CB00006B/2223